P9-APQ-843

COMMUNICATION SKILLS & STRATEGIES

Guidelines for Managers at Work

Jerry A. Dibble

Department of Business Communication Programs
College of Business Administration
Georgia State University

Beverly Y. Langford

Department of Business Communication Programs
College of Business Administration
Georgia State University

COLLEGE DIVISION South-Western Publishing Co.

Cincinnati Ohio

Acquisitions Editor: Randy G. Haubner
Production Editor: Sue Ellen Brown
Marketing Manager: Scott D. Person
Sponsoring Representative: George Erneston
Cover Designer: Mac Evans
Production House: WordCrafters Editorial Services, Inc.

EH63AA
Copyright © 1994
by South-Western Publishing Co.
Cincinnati, Ohio

ALL RIGHTS RESERVED
The text of this publication, or any part thereof, may not be reproduced
or transmitted in any form or by any means, electronic or mechanical,
including photocopying, recording, storage in an information retrieval
system, or otherwise, without the prior written permission of the
publisher.

2 3 4 5 6 7 MA 0 9 8 7 6 5

Printed in the United States of America

Library of Congress Cataloging in-Publication Data
Dibble, Jerry A.
    Communication skills and strategies : guidelines for managers at
work / Jerry A. Dibble, Beverly Y. Langford.
        p.   cm.
    Includes index.
    ISBN 0-538-83520-6
    1. Communication in management.   I. Langford, Beverly Y.
II. Title
HD30.3.D53   1994
658.4'15–dc20   93-50221

I(T)P
International Thomson Publishing

South-Western Publishing Co. is an ITP Company. The ITP trademark is
used under license.

PREFACE

WHY COMMUNICATION SKILLS MATTER

Today's business environment presents us with an increasingly complex set of circumstances. Global competition, the impact of new technology, and constant, rapid change have forced organizations to reinvent themselves and their corporate behavior. For individual employees, regardless of their job description, that means more attention both to communication skills and to strategies for applying them in the workplace.

Global Competition

Few could have foreseen at the beginning of the 1980s the pressure that global competition would put on U.S. business. Faced with challenges from multinational competitors, business organizations have had to become more flexible, more innovative, and more responsive to the marketplace. And managers have discovered the difficulty of responding to customers and managing operations across geographic and cultural boundaries.

In addition, rapid advances in technology, frequent changes in product design, and broader marketplaces mean that many managers no longer understand in detail the work their employees do or how they do it. Thus they depend on other people for information about the work they do and about customer response, new business opportunities, and market trends. Without strong communication skills, critical information can reach managers too late or not at all.

New Technology

Rapid change increases the flow of information, as does the communication technology most managers now have at their disposal. Unfortunately, neither necessarily increases the quality or the accessibility of the information. On the contrary, rapid advancements in communication technology over the past 10 years have swamped most managers with information they can no longer handle efficiently or pass along effectively.

The Changing Structure and Values of the Work Force

Changing attitudes toward work and more diversity in the work force mean that organizations must have employees with highly developed communication skills. Listening, probing for different points of view, hearing several sides of an issue on hard-to-solve problems—all are necessary for participative management to work and for employees to assume ownership of work objectives.

The waves of mergers, acquisitions, and downsizings that have swept U.S. businesses have made the problem worse. Flatter organizations, greater spans of control, and increased responsibility and accountability mean that managers must communicate in ways that foster teamwork and increase understanding of and commitment to company goals.

No wonder, then, that business leaders consistently point to effective communication as one of the two or three most important requirements for organizational and personal success. Clear, timely communication enables organizations to define themselves to their many constituencies: workers, regulatory bodies, customers, suppliers, stockholders, and the community at large. It is essential to motivating and empowering people, establishing new processes and systems, implementing more efficient operations, and ensuring organizational growth and vitality.

What This Means for You

In each case, the same issue presses down on U.S. businesses. If an organization hopes to create and sustain competitive advantage on the basis of its human and technical resources, it must find or develop managers who can communicate effectively.

For individuals the issue is no less pressing. Most business people can now look forward to six or more "careers" in their professional lifetime, each demanding different or expanded expertise. But communication skills—the ability to translate one's technical knowledge into clear, concise words and images—are fundamental to all careers and thus worth developing early and improving steadily.

HOW THIS BOOK CAN HELP

We wrote this book for students in the College of Business Administration at Georgia State University to help make sure they could communicate what they had learned in class. *Communication Skills and Strategies* is not a textbook. It is exactly what it says on the cover—a book of guidelines to help business people communicate more effectively. It covers everything from writing memos and letters to preparing presentations, making telephone calls, managing meetings, and working in groups.

HOW TO USE THE BOOK

Some people will decide to read the whole book or large sections of it before they try any of the material it contains. Others will read only the chapters that cover a specific upcoming project. Either approach is fine. We designed the book to be useful in desperate moments, not just on rainy evenings. *We suggest, though, that you read the material in this Preface before you use the book for the first time.* It will help you find what you need more quickly and make sure you don't miss important related material.

HOW THE BOOK IS ARRANGED

The sections following the Preface cover communication strategy, including planning and audience analysis. These sections contain key concepts that provide the foundation for material elsewhere in the book, so you should read them carefully, even if you have plenty of experience in these areas.

Following the sections on communication strategy are two large sections. The first covers written communication—memos, letters, and reports and the most effective ways to write and design them. The second covers spoken communication, including presentations, telephone skills, and meeting management.

HOW TO FIND WHAT YOU WANT

Each group of sections begins with a short introduction that outlines the characteristics of the medium and the way those characteristics influence your effectiveness as a communicator. The introduction to the section on written communication, for example, defines the six steps of the writing process. It then shows you how to manage them to avoid unnecessary work and maximize the message's impact on your audience.

The sections following the introductions contain the guidelines themselves. In all but two cases, we have limited ourselves to nine guidelines, fewer when possible. We have also tried to keep the guidelines process oriented. Material dealing with creating an agenda for a business meeting, for example, comes before suggestions on how to manage disruptive or counterproductive behavior once the meeting is under way.

The format should also help you find what you need. The guidelines are printed in boldface and are slightly larger than the rest of the text. In most cases, a paragraph or two follows the guideline to explain in more detail what the guideline means and how to apply it in business situations.

Some guidelines also include examples or commentary. Both are clearly marked so you can skip them if you are using the book for reference only or are in a hurry.

HOW TO GET THE MOST FROM THIS BOOK

We know from working with managers at many different levels that the techniques we recommend in the guidelines can produce dramatic improvements the first time you sit down to write a memo or plan a presentation.

More important, we believe that what you learn here will help you manage resources more effectively, make better decisions, and enhance your credibility and professional image.

We hasten to add that most of these miracles will not happen overnight. We recognize—and want you to recognize, too—that the way you communicate today, especially the way you manage spoken and interpersonal communication, results from years of experience. Neither our recommendations nor anyone else's can make permanent changes in that much learned behavior immediately.

Now for the good news. If you follow these guidelines consciously and systematically, you can expect them to pay increasingly rich dividends.

Here's how to make that happen: Don't try out everything at once. Instead, choose the area that you feel needs the most improvement and work on that until you get noticeable and consistent results. Then pick a new area to concentrate on. And then another and another. You will be surprised at how quickly committed, focused practice will produce lasting and significant rewards.

AND FINALLY ...

We would like to thank all of the business people, students, managers, and teachers who have contributed, directly or indirectly, to the material in this book. Without them, it would have been much more theoretical, less interesting, and far less useful.

We especially acknowledge the efforts of Dr. Veatrice Nelson, who contributed significantly to the project through her review, analysis, and suggestions for improving an earlier version of the text, particularly the sections on writing.

We also thank Michael Pursley for his contributions to the sections on spoken communication.

The reviewers' comments were helpful throughout and came at a time when we desperately needed fresh insight into the structure of the book. We wish to thank the following for a much-improved final product:

Robert E. Brown
Bentley College

James S. O'Rourke IV
University of Notre Dame

Geraldine Henze
LaGuardia College

Barbara L. Shwom
Northwestern University

Penny L. Hirsch
Northwestern University

John D. Stegman
The Ohio State University

John P. Leland
Purdue University

Particularly, we want to thank Jeanne Busemeyer and Sue Ellen Brown of South-Western Publishing for their continuing assistance.

We would like to enlist your help, too, by inviting you to tell us what topics you would like us to add, shorten, or even omit. Write or call either of us at the address below. We are always delighted to talk with you and are especially pleased when we can help readers with stubborn problems.

Jerry A. Dibble   *Beverly Y. Langford*

Business Communication Programs
College of Business Administration
Georgia State University
Atlanta, GA 30303-3083
404/651-1072

CONTENTS

PART ONE

THE COMMUNICATION PROCESS

Whatever the assignment or the pressure to get it done, the time you take to analyze the task, develop a strategy, and decide how to carry it out will pay high dividends.

In fact, five to ten minutes spent asking yourself explicitly about your objectives, how the audience sees the issue, and the relative merits of the different ways to deliver the message can literally save you hours of work. That is true whether you decide to write, call, or speak to others face to face. More important, a consciously developed communication strategy can help you recognize and take advantage of opportunities when they knock for the first and perhaps the only time. Developing a sound communication strategy also helps you avoid misunderstandings, bad feelings, poor decisions, and other undesirable outcomes.

But why develop a strategy when the situation is highly unstructured? What if you can't be sure what the audience will think, or in what kind of surroundings you will deliver your message? In fact, the less structured the situation, the more important strategy and planning become. Strategy and planning can help you make smart decisions under pressure. The more pressure, the more valuable they become.

The guidelines in this section present a simple, effective process that can help you no matter what kind of communication task you need to address. We think of the process as putting together a puzzle. You probably already recognize most of the pieces.

The first four pieces—Your Objective, Your Audience, Common Ground, and Appropriate Channel—play critical roles in assessing opportunities and developing an effective communication strategy. The next two—Best Evidence and Best Arrangement—come into play afterward. They concentrate on more tactical issues: what material to include in your message and how best to arrange it to meet the audience's needs and have the maximum effect.

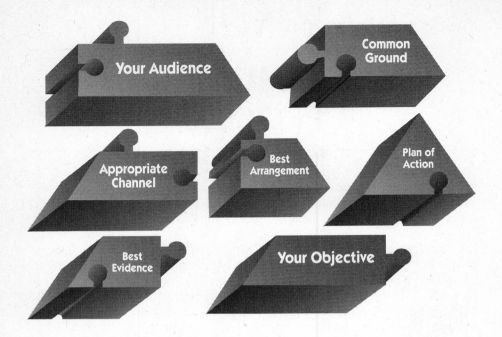

The final piece, the Plan of Action, engages the questions we all address when we sit down to execute the plan for delivering the message. What form should the message take? What is the most effective way to manage the process of writing, preparing a presentation, or conducting a meeting? We include this piece as part of communication strategy because managing the time you devote to implementing your strategy (doing things right) is as important as picking the right target and developing the best plan of attack (doing the right things). Separate sections of the book provide guidelines for managing each process.

DEVELOPING A COMMUNICATION STRATEGY

1. Determine your specific and general objectives.

Your Objective

Decide what you want your message to accomplish (specific objective) and how meeting this objective fits into your organization's strategic and tactical plans.

Most general objectives come from the organization's strategic plan. Managers then translate them into operational objectives for each functional area and within each functional area into specific objectives for individual projects.

A manufacturer's strategic plan, for example, may call for the firm to increase its market share by four percent and its profit margin by one percent. To realize those objectives, the marketing department may introduce several new products, engineering may commit to cut manufacturing costs on all products by one percent or more, and so on. Each set of decisions will result in communication of some kind—telephone calls, meetings, presentations, memos—and each communication will have a specific objective of its own.

Example

As a building manager, your specific objective is to convince the building owner to purchase a computerized security system for the building. This system will promote tenant safety and well-being and so fits with your company's general objective of maintaining high occupancy at premium prices.

3

Commentary

Most communicators fail because they don't identify their objectives explicitly and specifically. You must know what you want your audience to do after they receive your message and when, where, and how you want them to do it. Otherwise, you are likely to mistake action for results.

Almost everyone makes "to do" lists, but it would be much better if people made "to get" lists instead. "To do" directs attention to action; "to get" emphasizes achieving specific objectives—and that means starting with a clear idea of what you came to accomplish and a sure way to tell when you have finished.

2. Develop a clear and specific picture of your primary audience.

Your primary audience is the one person or group to whom you are directing your message. If you know your primary audience well, you can usually figure out quickly where they stand on the issue. If you do not know them well, start by asking these questions:

- What are your audience's general and specific objectives?
- Do they have hidden objectives that conflict with their stated objectives?
- How do their objectives relate to your message? How much do they already know about its subject matter? What opinions, if any, have they already formed about your recommendation?
- What is the audience's temperament? Is this an aggressive, bottom-line kind of individual or group, or do they make decisions slowly and methodically and pay attention to details each step of the way?

Example

The owner of the building is president of a small commercial development and property management firm. She earned an MBA five years ago and worked for a large accounting firm before forming her own company. The other decision makers in the firm come from a wide variety of backgrounds, including engineering and finance, but they are all numbers oriented and they make decisions carefully. Generally speaking, they would rather increase profit by operating more efficiently than by striking out into new territory.

Commentary

It is dangerous to generalize about people, but it is also dangerous not to. In most cases, making sound assumptions based on good information is better than making none and being unpleasantly surprised.

In the absence of specific evidence, do some homework. Find out about the fields the audience works in, about the firm and its history, which decisions its managers are most proud of, and what decisions they have made about related issues in the past. It takes a while to do all of this research, but not as long as it will take to go back a second time to get approval for your plan.

3. Base your primary message or statement of purpose on the common ground between your objectives and your audience's.

A good primary message or statement of purpose summarizes what you want to do and why the audience should care. It thus establishes the foundation for further communication on the topic and eventually an agreement about a specific course of action.

We think of a primary message this way. Imagine you are in an elevator on the 29th floor, and the two managers you most wanted to reach walk through the door. You know that they will get off at the 34th floor. The primary message is what you say between the 29th and 34th floors that makes them ask you to get off at 34 and tell them more about your idea.

You won't have time for more than one or two sentences. What you say must state clearly and concisely what you want to do and why your audience should care about it. If your message is on target, you get off at the 34th floor; if not, you go back to your desk to reconsider your strategy.

Example

"A computerized security system will improve our ability to protect our tenants and their property, making the building more attractive to tenants. It will also reduce our operating costs by lowering insurance rates and decrease the risk of costly lawsuits and legal fees."

Commentary

As you pitch the computerized security system to your employer, you know that you've got to create an issue that will offset her desire to avoid spending. You must zero in on the importance of keeping tenants so that the building remains profitable and on the cost of lawsuits should a tenant suffer property or personal damage. Your argument here is the cost of *not* purchasing the system.

4. Decide how hard a sell your audience will be.

You have probably been doing this all along, but it is a good idea to make a formal assessment. The difficulty of the undertaking will help you decide several important things, including how long the message should be, how persuasive it needs to be, and the best arrangement of material. Here are some considerations that can help you come up with an answer:

- **Your audience's probable attitude toward the topic.**

  - Will your audience be indifferent, skeptical, hostile, receptive, supportive?
  - What objections might they have?
  - Do you have good arguments and good evidence to offer when they raise their objections?

Example

The firm's managers worry about unoccupied space and the effect it has on the company's profitability and cash flow. They also worry about unproven or unreliable technology. Last year they computerized the heating and air-conditioning system to conserve energy and lower costs, but the system has never worked properly. Several tenants have threatened to break their leases if it isn't fixed soon.

To sell them your plan, you will have to show that the security system will work reliably. You will also have to show that investing money in the system will improve earnings in the long run, and your evidence will have to include numbers.

■ **Your audience's probable attitude toward you.**

Consider both the credibility of your position and your personal credibility. How long have you been on the job? What is your track record? What do people think of your boss?

If the audience is an external audience, how much do they know about your firm? Have they dealt with the firm in the past, and if so, what impression did the firm make?

If your credibility is low, or the risk of the recommendation is high, you may want to plan now to involve others as sponsors or champions.

Example

Although you have been building manager for only nine months, your employers hired you away from a competitor because of your excellent record. From the beginning, they have allowed you to run the building with little interference. They are comfortable with your competence. As long as you can back up your assertions, they will usually go along with your recommendations.

■ **Your personal communication style.**

Are you more comfortable with numbers or ideas? Do you approach a subject analytically or intuitively? Different communicators have different styles just as they have different strong and weak points. Knowing that your best style and the style the audience expects are not a good fit doesn't mean you should abandon the project. But it is worth considering when you calculate your odds of success and develop your plan of action for selling the recommendation.

5. Choose the most appropriate channel for your message.

- **Choose to write when**

  - Shelf life is more important than immediate feedback.
  - You need a permanent record of your message.
  - You need to send the message to large numbers of receivers.
  - You need to be sure the words are exactly right before you send the message.

When you choose to write, remember that feedback will be slow, even in the age of fax machines and electronic mail. You must compose and send the whole message before you know how the audience will respond to any part of it. Writing is therefore a poor choice for most open or sensitive issues.

However, in such a situation you might consider writing an invitation to an open discussion of the problem, accompanied by a brief summary of the facts as you know them. And of course, written follow-up is essential following delicate and potentially volatile discussions, such as performance reviews and disciplinary action.

- **Choose to speak when**

  - The issue is sensitive, with several sides, and each has its supporters (performance reviews and discussions of major business decisions are good examples).
  - You need immediate feedback.
  - You need to be sure your audience understands the message.
  - You need to deliver a message with maximum impact.

Commentary

Because you receive immediate feedback when you speak, you can adapt your message to the situation or to audience reactions quickly. This ability is especially important when the audience may have an immediate and emotional reaction to something you have said. It is also important if you suspect they may not understand something or will have questions about related issues.

Research shows that in face-to-face spoken communication, words alone are only 7 percent of the message another person receives. Inflection, tone, emphasis, and other vocal qualities account for 28 percent. The remaining 65 percent is nonverbal—eye contact, gestures, facial expressions, dress, and posture.

If you are often uncomfortable when you write, it is in part because writing can carry only about 10 percent of the message you would deliver in person. If you call someone on the telephone instead, you will deliver 35 percent of the message you could present in person. You will also have the advantage of an open feedback loop. But the feedback loop will carry only 35 percent of the information that you could get if you were there to watch the person's facial expressions, gestures, and other body language. That's why you may be uneasy handling difficult and emotional issues over the telephone.

■ **Choose a combination of channels when no single channel can provide all the qualities you need.**

In many cases, you may need the precision of written communication but the force and immediate feedback of spoken communication. In performance reviews, for example, open and personal communication is critical, but you must also have a written record of the discussion. Similarly, most professional communicators supplement presentations with a written report to reinforce the message and address the needs of secondary audiences.

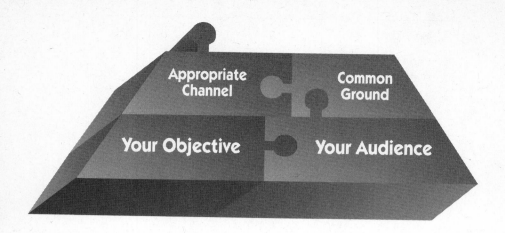

Regardless of the channel you choose, certain planning considerations appear in every situation. How you plan and prepare a written document, for example, has some steps in common with the way you plan and prepare a presentation. But keep in mind that writing and speaking differ in important ways and that the differences have important implications for the planning process. We will discuss the differences and their impact in more detail in the following sections of the book.

6. Select the best evidence for your argument.

Separate essential information from information that is merely nice to know. Include only the information the audience needs to make an informed business decision today.

Like everyone else, business people are inundated with information. Your most important task as a communicator is to help them focus their attention on the 10 percent of the available information that has the most impact on the decision they need to make today. Hold the other 90 percent in reserve for another time.

Example

You have solid information about discounts that your insurance company offers for protected buildings and can calculate the yearly savings and the payback period for the investment. On the other hand, it is not clear whether inadequately protected tenants will sue building owners. Because the evidence is inconclusive and will take a lot of explaining to show why, you decide to emphasize the first point. You will mention the second as an issue but not discuss it in detail.

If you believe that someone who reads your proposal may ask about the specific costs of legal action, you may want to include that information in an appendix. Similarly, if you plan a presentation, you may want to prepare backup visuals to use in responding to questions from the floor. In either case, however, you would exclude this material from the body of your proposal or presentation.

7. Select the best arrangement for the material.

Look for the most appropriate arrangement for the audience you are addressing today. Begin with the question that is uppermost in their minds. If they don't have a question in their minds, tell them what has changed and then address the question the change suggests. From there on, good writing and good speaking are like good conversation, with one question or statement leading to another.

If you know your specific objective and your audience well, you will usually find that the best overall arrangement for your message will already be clear, including the amount of time you ought to spend on each topic.

Example

Statement	**Audience Response**
The new municipal bond issue just failed.	So what?
It means less police and fire protection for our building, higher insurance rates, and more threats to tenants' safety.	That is serious. What can we do?
I've been looking into computerized security systems, and I think they may be the answer to our problem.	This isn't going to be like our "computerized" climate control system, is it?
No, certainly not. I've talked to several building managers who have this type of security system, and they give it high marks for reliability. (Some numbers to back up your assertion are appropriate here.)	Sounds good. How much does the system cost?
The initial investment is fairly high, but I have some numbers on the reductions in insurance premiums we could expect to see and the payback period on the net investment that I think you will find interesting.	

8. Develop a clear plan of action and follow it.

Both the written and spoken channels of communication present special opportunities for maximizing the payback on the time you spend in preparing your message. In the chapters that follow, you will discover specific guidelines for planning and preparing memos and other documents, planning and delivering presentations, and managing effective meetings and other communication tasks that require developed interpersonal skills. Each chapter is process oriented and, in addition to the guidelines, contains ideas to help you develop the skills to put them into practice.

PROJECT STRATEGY SHEET

What do you want to happen as a result of your communication? Focus on results by beginning your objective statement with "To get." Whenever possible, incorporate specific times, places, profit goals, and so forth. (Example: "To get final approval on revised budget for FY 1994, including positions for two new clerks, 4 percent increase in travel funds, and product training for all customer contact employees by June 1.")

What in your subject matter is new to your audience and why should they care about it? If your message will address more than one audience, answer the question for each audience. Try to imagine the audience's thoughts, questions, and expectations.

When possible, include quantitative information in your thinking—how often, how much expense, how much wasted time, how many lost customers, how much new business.

(continues)

14

Common Ground

What is the bottom line for you and your audience? Pull your thinking about the first two strategic elements into a one- or two-sentence statement. The statement should capture your objective and the most important reasons why the audience should give it their attention. (Example: "Our inventory costs have increased 20 percent over last year and will seriously compromise our profitability unless we get them under control now. I have two ideas I think will help.")

Appropriate Channel

What is the best medium for your message? Should you write, speak to a group or an individual, communicate face to face or over a telephone, or use some combination of media? In answering, consider the need for documentation, the audience's need to study the message, and the level of persuasion your objective requires.

PART TWO

WRITTEN COMMUNICATION

Very few people in business will tell you that they actually like to write. For many, the prospect conjures up unpleasant memories of high school English class. And even for those who like to write, deadlines and interruptions can make writing in a business environment a frustrating and laborious process. It's so much easier just to pick up the phone or call a meeting.

To complicate the matter further, the written communication channel is narrow, lacking all the visual cues that you depend on when you speak. All you have left are the words themselves and the way they appear on a page.

But every business person regularly encounters situations in which no mode of communication works as well as putting it in writing. The reasons are obvious: permanence, credibility, precision, and efficiency. Even in the age of electronic mail, videoconferences, and mobile telephones, hard copy still plays an important role in effective business communication.

The Writing Process

Since you can't avoid writing altogether, this section of the guidebook shows you how to create effective written messages in the minimum amount of time. It begins by examining the various steps in the writing process. It then shows you how to get the most out of the time you invest in each step and how to avoid getting bogged down and frustrated. It also demonstrates some important techniques for designing documents to make information more accessible to readers and for putting the finishing touches on completed documents.

MANAGING THE WRITING PROCESS

Efficient written communication depends on the writer's ability to manage each of the six steps in the writing process. The writing process begins with (1) an appropriate communication strategy and (2) a plan for executing it; moves through (3) drafting, (4) rough editing, and (5) fine editing; and ends with (6) proofing and correcting the completed document.

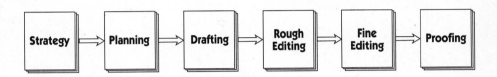

Trained writers address the steps one at a time, investing the most time in the steps that produce the highest return on their effort. Undisciplined writers, including most business writers when they are in a hurry, jump back and forth unnecessarily between one step and another. In the process, they often waste time and lose sight of their objective.

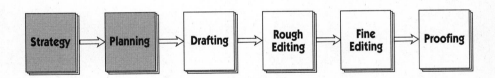

1. Take time to plan.

Of all the steps in the writing process, strategy and planning contribute most to the impact your message will have on its audience. If the strategy is wrong and the plan for executing it faulty, you can draft, edit, and proofread endlessly and you still won't improve your message enough to get the job done.

Paradoxically, strategy and planning are the steps that most writers shortchange. Instead of taking time to think about their audience and their objective, they jump right in to drafting, hoping that their message and the audience's needs will become clearer as they write and revise. Sometimes that happens, but most of the time hurried writers pay a high price for not taking time to plan. They revise their work time after time because it "just doesn't sound right," or they discover that other stakeholders had views and information they should have considered before they wrote anything at all.

As you plan, use the Project Strategy Sheet at the end of "Developing a Communication Strategy" to develop a preliminary appraisal of the opportunity you want to address. Then use outlining, clustering, or other planning techniques to create a working plan for the document.

2. Capture the audience's attention in the first paragraph.

Audiences always want to know two things first: what's new and why they should care about it. The more concretely you can answer both questions, the more attention your message will get.

Example

As manager of the office complex, you have decided to propose the computerized security system for the property. You begin by answering the "Why should I care?" question:

"Last week, a secretary leaving Park Centre office complex, not three blocks from our building, was accosted in the parking lot, robbed, and beaten. A month ago, burglars broke into the new Century Plaza complex and walked away with some $300,000 in valuable computer equipment. Both office buildings have lost tenants, and the Park Centre management group has been notified of pending legal action by the secretary and her employers."

One school of thought holds that audiences will be more receptive to your message—especially if it's bad news—if you take time first to walk them through the steps that led to your decision. We believe it is best to ignore such advice. In business, decision makers don't want to be kept in suspense or wade through mounds of detail to discover your message, so avoid building to a climax. Tell them what you recommend fast. Save the supporting detail, evidence, or rationale for the recommendation until you are under way.

CLUSTERING

Clustering, or "mind-mapping," can help translate your communication strategy into a working draft. Begin by writing the subject of the message at the center of a piece of paper. Draw a circle around the subject and then begin to jot down, around the circle, the results of your thinking about objectives and audience concerns. As you work, arrange related subtopics under the appropriate heading. Don't worry about neatness or the final arrangement of the material. The objective of the exercise is to create a "map" of your rough ideas and their relationships to each other.

Example

You must write a letter to a potential customer announcing a new UPC scanning cash register for small businesses. Your objective is an appointment to show the product, the Scansalot System.

As the sample cluster shows, you begin by writing the subject of the letter in the center of the page and drawing a circle around it. You then think of the various topics you will want to discuss:

- Advantages of the product over less sophisticated registers.
- Special promotional programs.

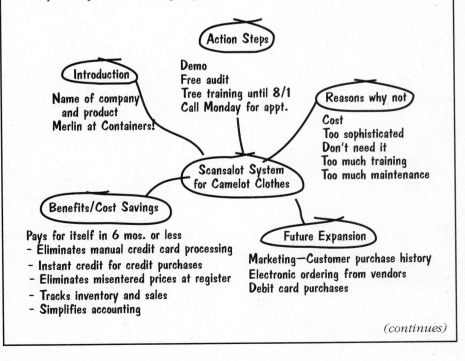

(continues)

- The range of models and pricing; reservations the owner may have.
- Another merchant in the same shopping mall who has just purchased the Scansalot System.
- An opportunity to meet with you to see a demonstration..

When the flow of ideas stops, ask about the starting point for your letter. Put a "1" next to the section of the cluster where you find the best opening material; then mark the remaining sections in the order you want them to appear in the letter. In the process, you may add or cross out material.

For example, you decide to open your letter with a reference to Merlin Williams, the manager of the Containers! store in the mall. As you continue to organize the map, you move next to the advantages of the system, in the process thinking of another plus: faster checkout during busy periods. You deal with objections only by mentioning positive features of the system. And finally, you list only one expansion possibility—the ability to track customer purchases—because it seems the most applicable for a clothing store.

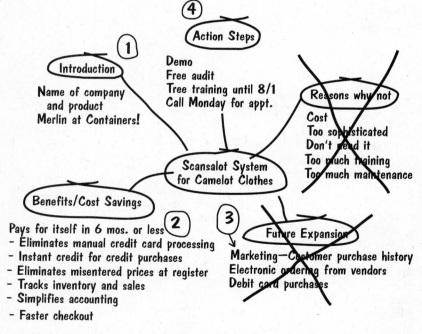

When you have laid out your plan, write the complete rough draft, using your cluster diagram as an outline.

(continues)

Scansalot

22 Criswell Drive, San Antonio, Texas 27867

Ms. Guinevere Jamison, Manager
Camelot Clothing
Ford Place Mall
Scottsdale, Arizona 00000

Dear Ms. Jamison:

Your neighbor, Merlin Williams, in the Containers! store recently installed our new Scansalot System registers. I encourage you to stop in and talk with him about them.

With the new registers, Merlin can now track revenues, inventory, and accounting data with 50 percent less effort than before. He can also process credit card purchases directly through the register, eliminate most of the paperwork, and get guaranteed immediate credit for the transaction. Finally, he has already found that Scansalot makes it virtually impossible to enter prices incorrectly and significantly speeds checkout during busy times of the day.

I would like to talk with you personally about the advantages this new system can offer Camelot Clothing. I think you will be especially interested in a new feature that can track customer purchases and alert them to new arrivals of merchandise they have purchased before. I will call next week to make an appointment. In the meantime, I hope you will have an opportunity to visit with Merlin and take a look at his new Scansalot System.

Sincerely,

Jim Pendragon

Jim Pendragon
Senior Sales Representative

P.S. Now is an especially good time to look at our Scansalot System, since we can offer free training for you and your employees on any system installed before August 1. By working carefully with Merlin, we were able to change over to the new system without any interruption of his normal business activities.

Example

"We need to purchase a computerized security system immediately to assure the safety of our tenants and the stability of our occupancy."

Next, fill in the remaining information, putting it in an order that anticipates the audience's concerns. In the case of the security system, that might mean addressing the benefits of the system you recommend:

- Its ability to ensure tenant safety and prevent burglaries.
- Its low cost relative to higher insurance premiums or lost tenants and unrented apartments.
- Its reliability (as demonstrated by references from managers of nearby buildings and by the vendor's quick-response maintenance program).

3. Always tell your audience what you want them to do.

Don't rely on the audience to decide what you want them to do. If you want a specific action, tell them. And don't settle for a weak, cookbook ending such as "Please don't hesitate to call if you have questions." (No audience today will hesitate to call with questions or concerns.) In general, as you conclude, focus on the attitude you want the audience to have when they finish your document.

Example

"The security system will provide everything we need at a price the firm can easily afford. I would like to have your approval today so we can negotiate a final price with the vendor and install the system during the holiday break."

4. In longer documents, provide preview paragraphs that describe what each upcoming section of the document is about.

Begin each section of the document with a preview paragraph that tells the audience what the section is about, how to use it, or how to find what they want. In planning the preview paragraph, ask yourself how the audience will use the document and answer this question: "How can I describe the material in this section so that the audience will know whether they need to read it and how to find key information quickly?"

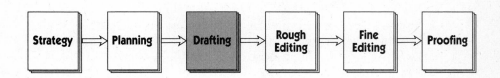

5. Draft the document according to your plan, without editing or rethinking your strategy.

When you have developed a strategy and a plan for putting it into action, you are ready to put pencil to paper or fingers to keyboard. The primary objective is a complete draft of your message that you can read and evaluate in light of your objectives for the communication.

In drafting, write your ideas down quickly so that they flow from one point to another. Concentrate on getting something down on paper that states your message concisely, makes your recommendations, answers any questions your audience may have, and tells them what you want them to do. Imagine that you are face to face with your reader, and write as though you were conversing with an equally intelligent individual. Don't use a lot of self-deprecating statements such as "In my opinion," "I feel," or "I think." Convey confidence. Use language appropriate for discussion between professionals. And don't clutter your message with official-sounding phrases you would never use in a real conversation, such as "Per your request . . ." or "Attached, please find . . . ."

You don't need to follow your outline slavishly, but don't stop to rethink your strategy either. If it's necessary to do that, you will have time later.

Don't mix drafting and editing. Most writers waste time in this step because they stop to edit the draft before it is complete, second-guessing the way they have chosen to express an idea or worrying about points of grammar and syntax.

Keep the pressure on yourself to write straight through without stopping. Doing so will help you avoid the temptation to add information that is merely nice to know but not essential. Also, you won't waste time trying to solve problems that don't need to be solved yet or improve sentences that may not survive the next draft.

Once you see the entire memo, letter, or report, you will be able to make better decisions about what to omit, rewrite, or add. Remember, sculptors don't chip a nose out of a huge block of marble and start polishing it. They begin by roughing out the entire figure to get a sense of the overall shape of the work and how the parts relate. Then they refine it. You should work the same way.

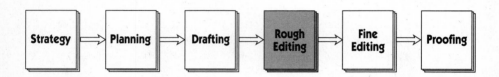

6. Check carefully for completeness and coherence.

When you have completed the draft, measure it carefully against your plan. Ask whether your draft answers the following questions:

- Have you told your audience what's new and why they should care about it?
- Does the sequence of topics achieve your objective and ensure your readers' understanding? Have you grouped similar subjects? And have you linked those groups in a way that anticipates and responds to the readers' needs and expectations?

  Transitions. Look at the flow from sentence to sentence and paragraph to paragraph. Have you supplied appropriate transition words or phrases so your readers can easily see the connections within and between paragraphs?

  Paragraphs. Test your paragraphs for length and coherence. Make sure that each paragraph is short and clearly focused on a single subject. On the average, paragraphs should be eight lines or fewer.

Excessively long paragraphs turn audiences off. Take a look at the next long paragraph you write. You will probably find that you can turn it into two or even three shorter ones.

- Have you told the audience what step, if any, you would like them to take as a result of reading your message?

If the answer to any of these questions is "No" or "I'm not sure," now is the time to fix the problem. Now is also the time to cross out unnecessary material or move paragraphs that would be more effective somewhere else.

On the other hand, don't make a career out of revising. Effective revisions at any level should produce 90 percent of the improvements on the first pass. Stay focused on changes at the paragraph level and above. Editing (revisions at the sentence level) will take place during the next step. If you try to do that here, you may waste time wordsmithing a sentence that may not make the final draft.

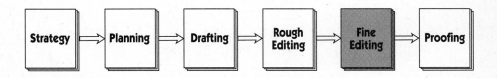

Editing at the sentence level for clarity and readability ensures that the document will convey your message with maximum impact. When you are satisfied that the organization of your document meets your objectives, use the following guidelines to edit for style and readability.

7. Write short sentences.

For most business writing, sentences should average 12 to 17 words, depending upon the experience and knowledge of your audience. The more technical the material and the less knowledgeable the audience, the shorter your sentences should be. (We thought this was obvious, but we have found that experts in all fields consistently use technical subject matter as an excuse for long sentences.)

When you find a sentence that is too long, you can shorten it in several different ways, depending on the reason for the excessive length.

- **Too many ideas.** Some sentences are too long because they contain not one but several related ideas. Readers can give important ideas the attention they deserve only if you give each idea a sentence of its own. Cramming several ideas into the same sentence will ensure that the reader doesn't pay sufficient attention to any of them.
- **Needless words.** Needless words take up space without contributing to the meaning of the sentence. In many cases, they clutter the sentence so badly that the audience can't find its meaning. Always cross out false starters such as "It is" and "There are" and empty phrases such as "The purpose of this document is to. . . ."

Examples

Wordy:	It is breeding that matters most to dog lovers.
Concise:	Breeding matters most to dog lovers.
Wordy:	There are three people who can sign this application.
Concise:	Three people can sign this application.
Wordy:	The purpose of this document is to establish guidelines for purchasing data processing equipment.
Concise:	This document establishes guidelines for purchasing data processing equipment.
Wordy:	The one area of sizable difference I felt I didn't have that much control over this year involved travel expenses.
Concise:	Travel expenses got out of control this year and severely impacted the budget.

- **Unbulleted lists.** Some sentences are actually lists of steps to take or points to remember. Do your readers a favor by using bullets to reveal the real character and mission of the sentence. A list helps your reader take in itemized information quickly and find it again later. This format works well for conclusions, recommendations, and other critical elements.

Example

Poor: Before preparing your proposal for a client, make sure you discuss the project with at least two executives of the client company, review related programs they are already using, and discuss price structure with your manager.

Better: Before preparing a proposal for a client, make sure you

- Talk with at least two executives of the client company.
- Review related programs they are already using.
- Discuss price structure with your manager.

Commentary

Always keep items in lists or steps in a procedure parallel—that is, make sure they are all commands, all questions, all complete sentences, all objects, and so forth. In the "better" list above, for example, each step begins with an action word ("Talk," "Review," and "Discuss") and takes the form of a command.

Examples

Not Parallel:

Portfolio Size

The basic level of the portfolio during FY 1993 will be $16,000,000 to $25,000,000. These levels will be maintained considering the following items:

- Legal requirements.
- Liquidity and risk level protection.
- What funds are available for investments.
- Pledging requirements.

(continues)

- The maximum size will depend on the amount not needed for other investment alternatives such as loans, fixed, assets, etc.

Parallel:

Portfolio Size

The basic level of the portfolio during FY 1993 will be $16,000,000 to $25,000,000. We will maintain these levels considering

- Legal requirements.
- Liquidity and risk level protection.
- Funds available for investments.
- Pledging requirements.
- Funds allocated for other investment alternatives such as loans, fixed assets, etc.

Not Parallel:

Reasons for establishing an on-site child care center

- Productivity
- Absenteeism is up 12 percent
- Improve morale
- It would be good public relations

Parallel:

Reasons for establishing an on-site child care center

- Productivity
- Absenteeism
- Morale
- Public relations

(continues)

Or better, with prominent action words and a clear focus on the benefits of establishing a center:

An on-site child care center will

- Increase productivity.
- Reduce absenteeism.
- Improve morale.
- Generate favorable publicity.

8. Write in the active voice.

The phrase *active voice* describes sentences in which the actor (subject) comes first, then the action (verb), and finally the receiver of the action (direct object). For example: "The general manager hired a new vice president for sales." Because active voice is the most direct and forceful sentence structure, it is best for all kinds of business communication.

The opposite sentence structure is the *passive voice.* In passive voice sentences, the receiver of the action comes first and the actor comes last. "A new vice president for sales was hired by the general manager." Some passive voice sentences omit the actor altogether. ("A new vice president for sales was hired.")

Although passive voice is sometimes useful, it is usually less effective than active voice because it adds words to the sentence and is harder for readers to understand. Use the passive voice only when the identity of the actor is unknown or unimportant to the sense of the sentence. If, for example, the building fire alarm went off, forcing everyone to leave the office unnecessarily, you might say, "The fire alarm was set off by mistake this afternoon." Of course, you could also say, "This afternoon, someone set off the fire alarm by mistake."

Examples

Passive: A status report on the project was submitted by the team leader.

Active: The team leader submitted a status report on the project.

31

| Passive: | The meeting was attended by all five supervisors. |
| Active: | All five supervisors attended the meeting. |

Passive:	The salesperson was fired by the sales manager.
	or
	The salesperson was fired. (No actor, so no one takes the blame.)
Active:	The sales manager fired the salesperson.

9. Choose strong verbs instead of relying on *is, are*, and noun-heavy sentences.

Verbs are the lifeblood of a sentence. When the action of the sentence gets lost in abstract nouns and weak *to be* verbs, the sentence loses strength. To keep the life in a sentence, use a strong verb rather than *is, are*, or *were* plus a noun. To unearth the strong verbs in your sentence, look for words that end in: *-ation, -al, -ment, -ness, -ity, -ure, -ance,* and *-ence.*

Examples

| Weak: | The vice president gave her authorization to the project team for the development of a video program. |
| Strong: | The vice president authorized the project team to develop a video program. |

| Weak: | The implementation of the rule necessitated a reassessment of policy. |
| Strong: | When the SEC implemented the rule, the brokerage reassessed its policy. |

| Weak: | Attribution is appreciated to the authors of the paper and to ITE if material from the Proceedings is used. |
| Strong: | If you use material from the Proceedings, please attribute it to the authors and to ITE. |

10. State your position in positive form.

Negatives tend to confuse your audience or make them unreceptive to your message. When you have to say "No," say it, but whenever possible, use a construction that emphasizes the positive.

Examples

Poor:	The procedure will not be ineffective.
Better:	The procedure will work.

Poor:	Do not use this procedure except in case of an emergency.
Better:	Use this procedure only in an emergency.

11. Use personal pronouns and specific details to create a real-world scenario for the audience.

The more concretely and specifically you direct your document to the audience, the better response you will get. For this reason, you should use personal pronouns, especially *you* and *we*, and provide specific detail so the audience can see how your message applies to their situation.

Examples

Poor:	A security pass may be obtained from this office only if the applicant has written authorization from his or her department head.
Better:	To get a security pass from our office you must have written authorization from your department head.

Poor:	Information is needed from at least 1,000 telephone calls to obtain a statistically accurate value to be used for the average call length.
Better:	To get an accurate value for the length of an average telephone call, you must sample at least 1,000 calls.

Commentary

Most of us learned in high school English and by example in the office that we shouldn't use *I* and *you* when writing. But when writers eliminate *I* and *you*, they usually end up writing in the third person or eliminating the subject altogether. That

(continues)

usually brings on passive voice, as in "The decision was made to raise your credit limit."

Remember, you are a human being communicating with other human beings. With all the emphasis on customer service, why write in a way that makes the situation less personal?

Commentary

Computer-based style checkers help you flag long sentences, spot passive voice constructions, and find short, direct alternatives for wordy phrases. Like other computer software, however, style checkers are helpful only if you use them intelligently.

We suggest that you select one or two guidelines that have the greatest potential for improving your writing. Using the style checker, correct only those errors and ignore the rest. You may even want to turn off the program's other style rules to avoid distractions.

Finally, we suggest that you run punctuation and spelling checks separately, after you have finished editing. (See the guidelines for proofreading that follow.) Separating the two steps will help you avoid being distracted by punctuation and spelling when you are trying to improve the directness and impact of the message.

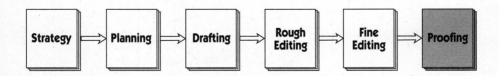

12. Proof carefully.

Managing the writing process includes attention to proofing, including checks on consistency of format, punctuation, spelling, and grammar. If your writing is 99 percent error-free, the offending 1 percent will still destroy the document's value, waste the time you invested in the project, and seriously damage your credibility. A mistake-riddled document delivers a single message that overrides everything else: The author didn't care enough to finish the project correctly.

At this stage, you should print the document. Text looks different on a sheet of paper than it does on a computer screen. Once you see it printed, you may want to consider changes in format. Also, check to make sure that spacing is correct and that line and page breaks are acceptable. If possible, have another person take a look at the document after you have checked it.

Ideally, two people should proofread together. If the piece is extremely important, you need to use this method. One reads from the final draft, while the other follows along on the copy that will go to the reader. If you don't have a proofreading partner, try reading the material backward so that you won't get caught up in the sense of the document and overlook errors. Especially be on the lookout for "typos" that create legitimate words—for example, *the* when it should be *they*. A computer spelling checker won't help you here.

Finally, remember to proof the nonverbal characteristics of the document as well as the verbal:

- **Check for consistency in format.** Be sure that you have used type sizes and styles, indentions, margins, spacing, and other formatting devices consistently throughout the document. Also make sure that illustrations and other graphics are properly located and identified.

- **Check for errors in spacing between words and sentences.** There should be one space between words and two spaces between the end of one sentence and the beginning of the next.

- **Check for unacceptable line and page breaks.** Avoid "orphans" (a short line at the top of a page), headings with fewer than three lines of text before the end of a page, and a final page with fewer than three lines of text.

Commentary

The rules of grammar exist to prevent misreading, avoid ambiguity, and eliminate confusion. You may be thinking, "My secretary handles all that." But secretaries miss work or quit, and in flat organizations, fewer managers have them. And even when you do have access to a secretary or administrative assistant, you are still the only one who knows exactly what you meant to say. For these reasons alone, you need to know what's right and to check for errors before you sign your name.

If you want to brush up on your grammar or just need to look up the answer to a specific question, refer to the Appendix, "General Tips on Punctuation, Grammar, and Usage." In it, we concentrate on the rules that give people the most trouble.

A FINAL WORD

Each step of the writing process contributes to the effectiveness of the final document. The better your plan for the document, the more effectively you will reach the audience. The better your revisions and the design of the document, the more easily the audience will process your message and the more impact it will have on their decision making. All six steps combine to produce effective writing, and each offers opportunities for improved clarity and directness.

DESIGNING READABLE DOCUMENTS

While most writers recognize the impact that good editing can have on the reader, few pay enough attention to *document design*—a term that includes everything from choice of format to selection of typefaces. It can add value to documents of all kinds, from short memos to book-length reports.

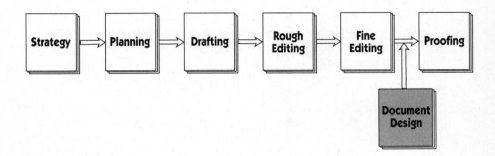

In the guidelines that follow, you will find material on creating effective headings, selecting the best font style and size, and using white space to emphasize significant divisions in the text. But the objective of all these techniques is the same: Men and women in today's workplace are inundated with information. For that reason, they seldom read more than 10 percent of any document that is more than two or three pages long.

Document design makes it easy for readers to find out what is included in your document and to find the part of it they want and need to read. Good editing makes it easy for readers to read what they need to know; good document design makes it easy for them to find what they need to read.

Some decisions about document design may take place during the planning step. The headings or categories in your cluster analysis, for example, may survive to become major or minor headings in the document itself. Or you may find that you can omit repetitive phrases such as "another major factor in our decision is . . ." by introducing each major factor with a subheading instead. Most decisions about document design, however, take place after you have completed your work on the document's text.

A well-designed document is not only easy to read; it also has a positive psychological impact on readers that translates into a positive attitude toward you and your message. In fact, document design can sometimes contribute as much to the message as the words themselves.

1. Create informative headings and subheadings.

Use headings to divide the document into logical units that are immediately understandable to readers. Maintain a reasonable balance between headings and text: Too many headings may interfere with the continuity of the memo or report; too few will leave large blocks of uninterrupted text that can intimidate readers and discourage them from reading what you have to say. Your readers can absorb information more readily if it isn't too densely packed.

Your design should emphasize important information and readily show the relationship between one piece of information and another. In short documents, you may need only one level of headings beyond the section title. In longer documents, you may need two or three. Except in rare cases, do not use more than three.

Example

MAJOR HEADING

Minor Heading

Subheading.   Embedded in the text or introducing a bulleted list.

Remember that headings and subheadings are signposts. Keep them brief and descriptive, but say enough that the audience will know what the section is about and whether it is worth their time to read it.

You can put headings in the form of questions that the section answers, questions the audience might have when they use the document, or summary statements of what the section says. When you select a form, use it consistently throughout the document.

Example

Note the difference between these two sets of headings for a proposal:

Too General	**More Informative**
Background	Your Request
Discussion	Our Approach What We Will Do How We Will Do It
Conclusion	The Benefits
Recommendation	The Next Step

2. Create a consistent, appropriate, and appealing design.

Good document design helps readers process information more efficiently by emphasizing important information and by establishing visually the relationship between one piece of information and another.

When writing for more than one audience, design the document for the audience that is least familiar with the material and provide fast tracks for those who are more knowledgeable. Here are some ways to do this:

- Provide a good index and table of contents for documents longer than 10 pages.
- Put key words in the margin or use informative headings to emphasize major points.
- Include illustrations to summarize key ideas or procedures.
- Consider preparing separate documents for each audience.

Examples

Ineffective Document Design:

Date: August 26, 199X   *Vague subject line*

Memo: Mary Forrester

From: Don Smitz   *Sans serif type*

Subject: Office Computer and Software

No informative headings

Right-hand margin justified

I have considered the criteria you gave me for the new computer. You said that the computer must be able to use the spreadsheets I created last summer and communicate directly with the mainframe. I also considered speed and expandability as major factors in developing my recommendation. Based on my research, I recommend that we purchase an IBM® PS/Value Point System and Microsoft® Excel™ software. In order to meet our criteria, the machine must have at least a 486SX microprocessor running at a minimum of 33 MHz, 8 megabytes of random access memory, a 120 megabyte hard disk, and the ability to run Microsoft Windows 3.1. The system must also be local area network capable. The major spreadsheets currently available for the IBM are Lotus® 1-2-3 for Windows™ , Version 1.1; Microsoft Excel for Windows, Version 4; and Quattro Pro for Windows, Version 1. The packages are comparable as to speed and power, and all can read the Lotus G™ spreadsheets that run on the mainframe. However, Microsoft Excel is currently the most adaptable to the Windows environment.

Embedded list

The total cost for hardware and software is approximately $2,000. Please review my comments and call me as soon as you decide. I am anxious to get our spreadsheets converted to Excel and start enjoying the increased speed and efficiency. I'm sure you are too.

Paragraph too long

MEMORANDUM

DATE: August 26, 1993

TO: John Caprioti

FROM: Don Smitz *DS*

SUBJECT: Recommendation for New Office Computer
and Software

I have considered the criteria you gave me for the new computer. You said that the computer must be able to
- Use the spreadsheets I created last summer.
- Communicate directly with the mainframe.

I also considered speed and expandability as major factors in developing my recommendation. Based on my research, *I recommend that we purchase an IBM®
PS/Value Point System and Microsoft® Excel™ software.*

How I Chose the Computer

In order to meet our criteria, the machines must have
- A 486SX microprocessor capable of running at a minimum of 33 MHz.
- 8 megabytes of random access memory.
- A 120 megabyte hard disk.
- Ability to run Windows™ 3.1.
- Local area network capability.

How I Chose the Software

The major spreadsheets currently available for the IBM system are
- Lotus® 1-2-3 for Windows™, Version 1.1.
- Microsoft Excel for Windows™, Version 4.
- Quattro Pro for Windows™, Version 1.

The packages have comparable speed and power, and all can read the Lotus G™ spreadsheets that run on the mainframe. However, Microsoft Excel is better adaptable to the Windows environment.

What Is the Next Step?

The total cost for hardware and software is approximately $2,000. Please review my comments and call me as soon as you decide. I am anxious to get our spreadsheets converted to Excel and start enjoying the increased speed and efficiency. I'm sure you are, too.

Commentary

Make your document reader friendly. At a glance, the audience should be able to see how the document is organized, where they are in the document, which items matter most, and how the items relate.

A good design creates a sense of order and encourages a positive attitude toward you and your message. Your readers should be able to find what they need quickly and painlessly.

3. Use white space and type selection to create a readable, attractive page design.

A page of unrelieved typewritten text is intimidating and uninviting. Design each page to make the document easier to read. Be sure the design is clear and consistent. Here are some elements to consider:

Paragraph Length

Visually, paragraphs should not be deeper than about two inches. (The preceding paragraph is less than an inch.)

Typeface

Typeface (also called *font*) means the style of type. Fonts fall into two broad categories: serif and sans serif. Serif, which has a fine line at the top and bottom of each letter, is the more readable in text. Sans serif, without fine lines, is crisp and clean and is usually appropriate for headings and visuals.

Within these categories you can choose from hundreds of typefaces. Some popular and readable serif fonts include Times Roman and New Century Schoolbook. For sans serif type, try Helvetica or Optima.

Serif type:	This is Times Roman.
Sans serif type:	This is Helvetica.

Type Size

For text, use 12 point type when possible and nothing smaller than 10 point. Use 14 point when you want to emphasize high-level headings and key words. Reserve the larger point sizes for headlines on newsletters or type on overhead transparencies.

Example

This is 10 point.

This is 12 point.

This is 14 point.

This is 18 point (minimum for overheads).

Indentations and Line Length

In typewritten or word-processed material, indentations vary from two to five spaces, depending upon the line length of the text. The longer the line, the longer the indentation. Place increasingly subordinate ideas and headings increasingly farther from the left margin, at intervals of no more than one-half inch.

Very long lines (more than seven inches) or very short ones (less than three inches) are hard to read. The best line length is five to six inches. The text on this page is about five inches, or about 65 characters long.

Margins

Allow generous margins (at least one inch) at the top, bottom, and on each side of the page. Except for typeset or desktop-published text, choose unjustified (ragged) right-hand margins over justified ones. Justified right-hand margins can distract the reader by creating abnormally large spaces between words.

Bullets

When using bullets or hyphens, align them with the start of the text above; then align the first words of each listed item.

Example

After the first of the year, we will expand our audiovisual department. Specifically, we plan to

*   Purchase Freelance Plus™ to format graphics for video output.
*   Purchase dissolve units in order to do multiple projector shows.
*   Hire another audiovisual specialist.
*   Hire a computer graphics specialist.

Commentary

Don't use more than two typefaces in a document; if you do, your page will look like a ransom note. Instead, add emphasis by using white space together with a larger type size, upper case, boldface, or italics.

Use bullets rather than numbers for lists, unless the items comprise a sequence. When an item runs over into the next line, either skip lines between all bulleted items or indent the second line.

Limit lists to five items or fewer. If you need to present lengthier information for reference, put it in an appendix or a table.

4. Use highlighting techniques to emphasize the organization of the document.

Within the typeface you choose, you have several ways to highlight important ideas and call attention to the organization of the document. As with headings, you should select a pattern and stick with it. Here are some possibilities:

Boldface

Boldface is the most effective way to emphasize a word, phrase, or sentence. For longer passages, it is too intense for most readers. Instead, add emphasis with solid lines above and below the passage or a box around it.

Italics

Italics are the traditional method of adding emphasis to words or phrases in printed material. Today, many writers use boldface instead. Use italics sparingly, to emphasize a word, phrase, or short sentence.

Underlining

Underlining can also be effective to highlight words or short phrases. Don't underline sentences or longer passages; long lines of underlined type are difficult to read.

Line Spacing

Use line spacing to separate units of text and emphasize design elements. In general, the more spacing, the greater the division and the more important the heading that accompanies it.

CAPITALS

Use capitals for section headings or to highlight a word, but not for long statements. Using all uppercase letters slows reading time by about 15 percent and takes up about 30 percent more space than lower-case letters.

Solid Lines

Use solid lines above and below or around important sentences or blocks of text to emphasize them.

Commentary

Computers and sophisticated word processors can greatly enhance your ability to design documents. However, you can also create a well-designed page using a typewriter. Remember that the primary objective of document design is to help readers find important information quickly, either on the first reading or on returning to the document later. Even a typewriter can accomplish that objective through intelligent use of spacing, underlining, and other simple techniques.

A word of warning. Excessive use of highlighting techniques can detract from your document's appearance and make your message more difficult for the reader to process. If you have a sophisticated desktop publishing system, resist the temptation to go overboard with highlighting.

5. Use appropriate graphic devices.

Graphics attract attention and can make information more accessible to the reader. A well-chosen and well-designed visual can often take the place of pages of textual explanation and make data relatively simple and easy to grasp.

Example

Written Explanation:

Who Must Sign Applications

Applications, amendments thereto, and related statements of fact required by the Commission shall be personally signed by the applicant, if the applicant is an individual; by one of the partners, if the applicant is a partnership; by an officer, if the applicant is a corporation; or by a member who is an officer, if the applicant is an unincorporated association. Applications, amendments, and related statements of fact filed on behalf of eligible government entities, such as states and territories of the United States and political subdivisions thereof, the District of Columbia, and units of local government, including incorporated municipalities, shall be signed by such duly elected or appointed officials as may be competent to do so under the laws of the applicable jurisdiction.

Graphic Equivalent:

Who Must Sign the Application	
TYPE OF APPLICANT	**SIGNATURE REQUIRED**
Individual	Personal signature
Partnership	One of the partners
Corporation	An officer of the corporation
Unincorporated Association	Member who is an officer
Government Unit	Appropriate elected or appointed official

Use graphics, however, only when they express important points more clearly or forcefully than text alone. Make sure that your visuals clarify, not just decorate, your document.

DESIGNING VISUALS

Well-designed illustrations and visuals are far more important than most people think. In an increasingly global economy, businesses depend more and more on visual information in the decision-making process. Obviously, the fewer words the message contains, the less translating multinational corporations must do.

But research shows that even for firms who do business in a single language, reading has become a luxury they can't afford. Most people read less than 10 percent of any document longer than two pages. As a result, illustrations assume an increasingly important role in summarizing and communicating important information.

Today, computer graphics programs allow communicators to prepare sophisticated charts, graphs, and diagrams and integrate them into their work with relative ease. But unless you use these tools effectively, the illustrations and visuals you create may decrease rather than increase the impact of your message.

1. Use a visual only where it will help you make a point more clearly or persuasively than text alone.

Visuals are important tools for improving communication, not mere aids or supplements. Use visuals to condense and clarify text, not to decorate it.

2. Limit each visual to a single, clear point.

Keep visuals simple and uncluttered. Design two simple visuals rather than trying to make a second point with the same one.

Unnecessary details ("chart junk" such as grids, cross-hatching, and three-dimensional effects) create the same problems in visuals that unnecessary words create in sentences and paragraphs.

3. Choose the most appropriate visual for the message and the use your audience will make of it.

Different kinds of visuals offer distinct advantages and disadvantages. Make sure that you pick the type that makes your point best.

Tables

Use tables to organize and show the significance of data, not merely to list it.

Tables are the least visual of all visuals. Best are informal tables that show a simple trend or a significant relationship between two variables.

If your assignment calls for tables that show more than two or three columns and ten rows, consider putting them in an appendix.

Some formatting hints:

- Begin each row and column with a brief caption that identifies the items listed and their units of measure. If you have long captions or more than three columns, stack the headings to save space.
- Help the reader's eye move from left to right or pick out significant data by using leader dots, shaded rows, extra white space between rows, and other visual devices.

Five-Year Forecast for Corrugated Sheets (with Estimated Production)

	Year 1	Year 2	Year 3	Year 4	Year 5
Total Market (millions of sq. ft.)	146	153	161	170	170
Total Market ($ millions)	$9.8	$10.8	$11.9	$13.2	$14.6
Market Penetration	16.0%	27.0%	42.3%	43.2%	43.3%
Estimated Production ($ millions)	$1.6	$2.9	$5.1	$5.7	$6.3

Bar Graphs and Column Graphs

Bar and column graphs help viewers compare the values of different quantities, such as sales by product.

A stacked bar or column graph shows the values of different components of the whole stacked one on top of the other instead of side by side.

- When designing either type of graph, use darker bars to represent the most important quantities.

- To represent the relationships between the quantities accurately, keep the bars the same width, and start the scale at zero.

Column Graph
Sales by State
1988–1992

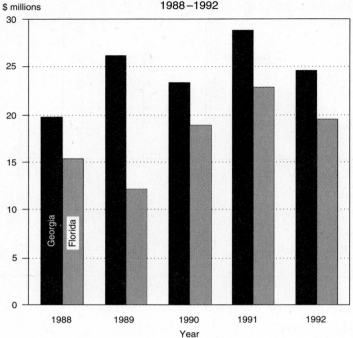

Stacked Bar Graph
Sales by State
1988–1992

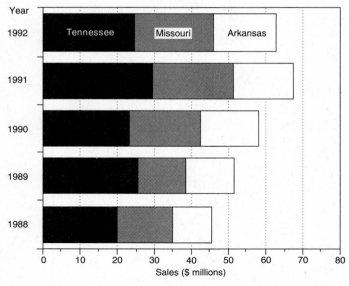

Line Graphs

Line graphs show how one quantity changes as a function of another—for example, how sales increase or decrease with time or how price changes with demand. These graphs accommodate many more data points than a bar graph and thus are better at showing trends.

Readers find line graphs harder to interpret than bar graphs. Take time to introduce and explain them, including the variables shown on the X and Y axes and the general trend the information describes.

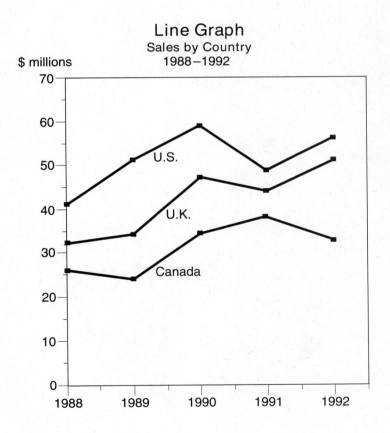

Line Graph
Sales by Country
1988–1992

Pie Charts

Pie charts are a good way to illustrate the size of one or more segments relative to the whole. They are *not* as good as bar graphs for showing the differences between one segment and another.

If one wedge is more important than the others, put it at 12 o'clock; otherwise, put the largest wedge at 12 o'clock and the remaining ones clockwise in descending order of size.

Limit the chart to two to five wedges; combine smaller segments under "Other."

For added emphasis, explode the most important section of the pie chart away from the rest of the graph.

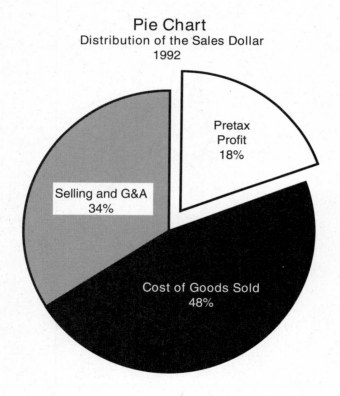

Pie Chart
Distribution of the Sales Dollar
1992

Pretax
Profit
18%

Selling and G&A
34%

Cost of Goods Sold
48%

Photographs and Drawings

Use photographs only when the actual visual appearance of the object is important. Otherwise, choose a drawing.

Unlike photographs, drawings allow you to be selective about detail and angle; they can also show objects in special ways (cutaway, exploded, etc.).

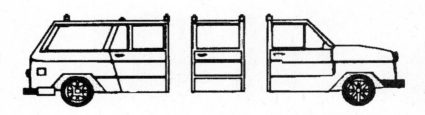

Diagrams

Use diagrams (including flow charts, organization charts, troubleshooting charts, and logic trees) to show the relationship among steps in a process—physical or mental—or between entities and concepts.

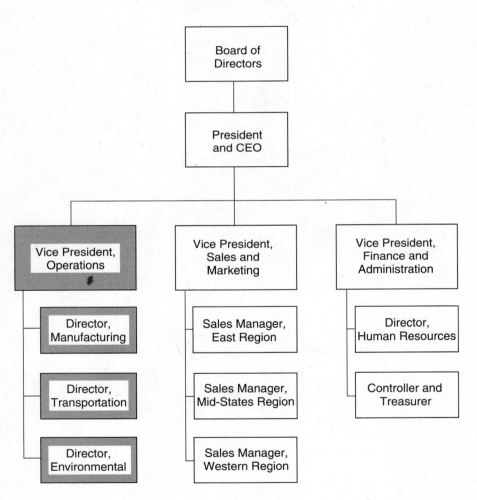

Organization Chart
Laurels Mattress Co., Inc.

4. **Always introduce the visual in the text; tell the reader where to find it and what to find in it.**

Put visuals where the reader can find them easily, on the same or an adjoining page whenever possible. Reprint a visual rather than asking a reader to remember it or turn to another page to find it.

Don't assume the reader will understand the visual's significance without your help.

Examples

As Figure 3 shows, sales were up for the third quarter in a row.

Sales at Acme were up for the third quarter in a row, but profits continued to drop. See Figure 3.

Sales were up for the third quarter in a row (Figure 3), but profits continued to drop.

5. **Make the visual easy to read and understand.**

- Label the important content clearly. Use arrows and color to call attention to significant details or variables. Always show units of measure for both numerical and non-numerical data. Label fields, and use color or varying shades of gray to distinguish them from each other. Do not use similar shades or colors in adjacent fields.

- Give the visual a clear, informative title. In a document, number it for reference.

- Always process data for the reader. Calculate percentages if they are important; arrange variables in a way that makes sense to the audience.

- Make the visual large enough that it can be read easily, but not so large that it overwhelms the page.

- As a rule, avoid cross-hatching to distinguish one field from another, and don't make the viewer use a legend to sort out the various cross-hatches.

- Use consistent typefaces, styles, and sizes, but limit yourself to two. Using more makes the visual look cluttered.

- Use plenty of white space to set the visual off from surrounding material.

PART THREE

SPOKEN COMMUNICATION

About 90 percent of day-to-day business communication is spoken. For every memo, letter, or report you write, you probably participate in dozens of meetings, conversations (both over the telephone and in person), presentations, interviews, and other spoken events.

Unlike the written channel, the spoken communication channel is broad, flexible, and adaptable. Besides the words you speak, your body language, gestures, voice inflection, rate of speech, eye contact, and facial expressions help convey your message. In addition, you receive immediate and continuous feedback from your audience so that you can adjust your message as you speak—even in mid-sentence if necessary.

Because spoken communication delivers so much more than the words you speak, it offers enormous potential to increase the impact of your message. Unfortunately, it has the same potential to destroy. The difference between success and failure usually lies in how well you plan what you are going to say and how effectively you manage the additional verbal and nonverbal messages that enter the channel.

COORDINATING NONVERBAL COMPONENTS

The challenge lies in managing the various nonverbal components so they reinforce rather than conflict with the meaning of your words. A pause can increase your authority, but not if you have just said something silly. And standing or sitting in a way that says you are an important person is useful only if you remember to breathe so that your voice doesn't shake or sound breathy.

Creating a unified, effective impression when you present or speak less formally takes many hours of effort. How you speak and how you manage nonverbal communication today are the result of years of practice, tutored and untutored, and much of what you do is subconscious. You can't realistically hope to change your behavior significantly over a weekend or even before the end of the month. Instead, resolve to work on one component at a time, preferably the one you believe will make the most improvement in the impression you make. Stay with it until you can see clear, sustainable improvement; then move on to another.

KEY COMPONENTS

When we analyze videotape or coach speakers, we usually talk about three key qualities of effective spoken communication: credibility, enthusiasm, and sensitivity to the audience. If you call to mind highly effective spoken communicators you have known, you will recognize that they project all three qualities.

Credibility

Unless you have done your homework and have some legitimate claim to expertise on the subject, you can't hope to inspire much confidence or credibility. But expertise alone is not enough. You must also manage the verbal and nonverbal components of your speech so that they support the intrinsic value of your message.

To communicate credibly, you must speak crisply and deliberately, with frequent pauses for breathing and relaxation. You must also be comfortable enough with your audience and your subject matter that you can stop to consult your notes, check your watch, or re-position an overhead transparency without becoming flustered or looking like you are afraid of losing the audience's attention.

Finally, you can increase your credibility by standing or sitting erect but comfortably. Placing hands in your pockets or leaning to one side, propping your chin on your hand, or shifting your weight from one foot to another all detract from your credibility and your image of confidence and control. (You may want to give up some control intentionally—for example, at the end of a formal presentation as you move to a question-and-answer session. Too much authority can discourage the audience from taking a more active role in the proceedings. But giving up credibility unintentionally lowers the audience's confidence in you and in the importance of your message.)

Enthusiasm

Effective communicators generate excitement about their subject matter—not by talking fast but with gestures, facial expression, emphasis, and tone of voice. Enthusiasm is drama appropriate to the subject matter of the communication.

Most speakers fall short of the best level of excitement for the subject matter because they are afraid of overacting, just as most speakers diminish their credibility because they lack confidence in themselves and the value of their message. If you want to experiment with techniques for increasing enthusiasm and credibility, try to include too much drama and too many pauses: it's hard for most speakers to do either, and the effort will bring you closer to the right levels of performance.

Commentary

Musicians and actors know that they often must exaggerate phrasing and dynamics to the point where neither sounds good to them as listeners. By the same token, you must often be far more dramatic, more forceful in your gestures and the way you use your voice than seems natural. If you aren't, the audience may see you as bored or apathetic—about the material and about them.

Sensitivity to Audience

In Western cultures, audiences derive much of their sense of contact with the speaker from direct eye contact. But you can also demonstrate your sensitivity to the audience and its concerns in other ways—by the way you dress, by responding to signs of confusion or disagreement, or simply by recognizing when the audience has had enough and is ready for you to stop talking.

If you call to mind effective communicators you have known, you will probably find that they have all managed to weave the three components together into a style that is highly effective and very distinctly their own. The goal, then, is not to reach a prescribed mix of the three qualities but to find the mix that is right for you, for your work environment, and for the subject matter of the spoken communication.

To create an effective blend of the three key qualities, you must first manage nervousness. Otherwise, your adrenaline level, not you, will control your speed of delivery and other important aspects of your message. The remainder of this introduction looks briefly at controlling nervousness, whether it is during a presentation, a job interview, or simply speaking up at a meeting to share an idea on an important topic. Then the guidelines that follow present specific techniques for managing different types of spoken communication—making presentations, using the telephone, managing meetings, and handling questions and answers.

MANAGING NERVOUSNESS

Most of us experience some nervousness when we have to communicate with a group, even a small one. Quite often, even an audience of one can make us uneasy—when it's time to ask the boss for a raise, for example.

Some nervousness can actually work to your advantage: your body creates adrenaline; the adrenaline increases your energy level; and you can actually perform better because you are a bit on edge. In many cases, however, the same chemical reaction can become debilitating, manifesting itself in a dry mouth, sweaty palms, a runaway pulse rate, and shaking knees. Until you control these extreme reactions, you can't do any of the other things that you need to do to be effective as a communicator— as a presenter, in a face-to-face conversation, or in a meeting, interview, or telephone call.

When you are nervous, tension in your muscles makes it hard to gesture naturally, hard to give your voice its natural resonance, hard to breathe— and, yes, hard to remember what you want to say next. To control nervousness, you need to relax both mentally and physically.

Relaxing Mentally

Many times we become nervous because we think too much about ourselves and not enough about the audience and the value of the topic and our ideas for them. As a result, we often conjure up images of grotesque personal failures or set grandiose and unrealistic expectations for our performance. Is it any wonder, then, that when things don't go well we begin to panic, convinced that the audience rejects our ideas and disapproves of us personally?

To avoid such unpleasant experiences, resolve to judge the outcome of the event not by how flawlessly you perform but by *how much value your audience receives.* The change will work wonders. You will focus on the audience and its needs instead of your own nervousness. You will also redefine success. If you do your best and your audience learns something valuable, the outcome will be successful even if you forgot something you planned to say or missed an opportunity to make an important point.

In short, seeing yourself as the servant of the audience is your single most powerful weapon against nervousness and the best insurance against failure and embarrassment.

Relaxing Physically

Mental and physical relaxation go hand in hand. When you are relaxed physically, you can think more clearly and respond more quickly to signals from your audience. On the other hand, if your body works against you by making you tense and uncomfortable, you will find it difficult to focus on your audience and your objective. And most of us make ourselves uncomfortable by the way we stand and sit.

You can take entire courses on relaxation and stress management, and we recommend them highly, especially if you need special help with nervousness or with physical problems such as back trouble or breathing disorders. For those without the time or need for such training, we generally focus on two simple rules:

1. Avoid postures that create physical tension.

2. Remember to breathe correctly.

Select the Most Comfortable Posture. If you are standing, keep your feet comfortably far apart. Distribute your weight evenly; then lean forward slightly so your weight just starts to come up on the balls of your feet. (If you lean backward, your knees will lock and send tension up your back to your neck and shoulders. If you put more weight on one foot than the other, you will shift your weight from one side to the other, tiring you and distracting your audience.)

When you are not gesturing with your arms, let them hang comfortably at your sides. Do not lock them behind your back, fold them in front of you, lock them in front of you in the fig leaf position, or tie them up by clutching a handful of notes or a ballpoint pen. All of these postures are uncomfortable and far less attractive than simply letting your arms drop to your sides.

To stay physically relaxed, stop after you make each point, take a breath through your mouth, relax your arms, and make sure your posture is still good. Remember that "good" is not ramrod straight—the way your mother and the third grade teacher told you to stand—but relaxed, with your weight properly distributed and the tension out of your neck and shoulders.

If you are in a meeting, in an interview, talking on the telephone, or making a presentation while seated at a table, sit with both feet on the floor and your arms resting comfortably on the arms of the chair or the edge of the table. Let the bottom of the chair take the weight of your body and the floor take the weight of your feet and legs. Any other posture, especially slouching in the chair or leaning to one side or the other, will make you uncomfortable. And physical discomfort quickly translates into mental tension. If you doubt this, just remember the last time you tried to perform a difficult or unpleasant task when you had a headache or were working in an overheated room.

Remember to Breathe Deeply. It seems silly to remind people to breathe, but breathing deeply is the first thing most people forget to do when they are nervous. They end up taking little short breaths that originate in the bronchial tubes rather than at the bottom of the lungs. As a result, their voices get shaky or breathy, they feel as if they are suffocating, and their brains starve for oxygen. Not surprisingly, they can't remember what they wanted to say next—and they won't until they breathe correctly.

In the following pages, you will find guidelines for managing the full range of spoken communication—not just formal and informal presentations, but also effective telephone calls and more productive meetings. As you read the sections, remember that they are interdependent. The things you learn about using your voice in "Using the Telephone Effectively" transfer directly to using your voice effectively during presentations or during a decision-making meeting. The same is true of other spoken communication skills. In each case, your improved ability to manage both the verbal and nonverbal components of your message will pay large dividends in the force of your message and your personal confidence.

MAKING EFFECTIVE
PRESENTATIONS

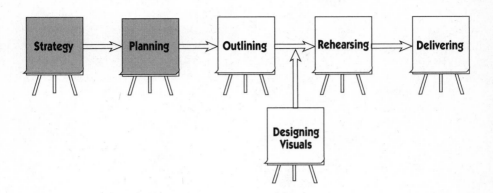

Designing a presentation involves many of the same steps as preparing a written document. First, you must identify your objective, the audience, and the common ground between your purpose and their needs. When the presentation is over, if you accomplish your purpose, what will happen? Will you get the go-ahead on a new project? Will a prospective client give your firm the nod? Perhaps the CFO will approve funding for a much-needed piece of lab equipment.

Again, as with written communication, you must decide why your audience should care about your subject. Try to imagine the decision makers' concerns, needs, and expectations as they listen to your presentation. What do they want? What do they know already? What are their most significant objections or fears?

Example

Suppose you are designing a corporate presentation that everyone in your company from sales representatives to vice presidents will use when contacting a potential client. Most firms begin, incorrectly, by inundating the audience with information about the company: when it was founded, how many branch offices it has, how many employees. But potential customers want to hear first how well your company understands their needs and how effectively it can meet them. Does your prospect's company need help in increasing sales, allocating resources, improving a process or a system, or developing a benefits package? Your audience must know immediately that you understand their critical issues.

In planning your presentation, you can use the same general process that you used for written communication. Just remember that listeners differ from readers in many important ways.

For one thing, listeners don't have visual clues such as headings, paragraphs, and white space to help them keep track of where they are and where they are going. Consequently, you must take extra care to design spoken messages so listeners can follow your ideas without confusion or misunderstanding. As you plan your presentation, then, provide a clear roadmap for the audience by stating up front the major divisions of the presentation. Support your words with appropriate visuals and a clear rationale for the arrangement of material.

Second, remember that a presentation offers a multitude of opportunities to take advantage of the nonverbal qualities of spoken communication. Too many times presentations become only a spoken version of a written document: a report, a proposal, or a memo. As a result, we present more information than the audience can absorb, or, if we have the document in front of us, we end up reading it—a surefire way to lose an audience.

Commentary

Presentations should have fewer main points and subtopics than written reports, and they should be less complex. Research on written material shows that readers tend to become confused when they try to absorb more than five to nine "chunks" of information at a time. In spoken messages, the maximum number of chunks is probably three to five.

A well-structured presentation should have no more than two or three main points and no more than two or three subtopics or bullets under each major point. If you find more, drop the least important or create a new topic.

1. Identify your objectives.

Be sure that your objectives are clear and specific, that you know your audience, and that you use your information about the audience to create the best design for your presentation.

Example

Your management consulting firm, Training Synergies, Inc., specializes in team building, conflict management, management by objectives, and total quality management. You are preparing a presentation for a potential client that will demonstrate how your company can help his management team achieve higher performance through cooperation.

Your audience is the CEO of HomeCare Manufacturing Company, a 15-year-old privately held firm that manufactures health care products for the home. The company has a reputation for being highly profitable but tough on its employees. The CEO, who built the company from a small operation in his garage, has told you that the company has been bombarded by competition. During the last three years, its share has dropped from 45 to 36 percent.

Personnel turnover at all levels is high, and those who leave HomeCare usually go to work for a competing company. In addition, the employee union, which for a number of years was fairly dormant, has begun to assert itself.

Your firm has already prepared a comprehensive report, assessing the needs of the corporation, formulating a strategy for solving its problems, and proposing a plan to implement this strategy. You will base your presentation on the most important contents of that report. If your presentation is successful, the CEO will give your company the go-ahead to proceed with the project.

Commentary

When you're planning, be sure that spoken communication will best meet your objectives, and if so, determine what type of spoken communication is most appropriate. Remember that a formal, stand-up presentation is very close to a report or memo in one respect: It allows the audience relatively little opportunity to air their views. But it differs from a report in that you simply can't present as much information, and your audience won't have the opportunity to refer to various points or reread at leisure. You must distill the most compelling ideas and adapt them to the new arena and medium.

(continues)

In some cases—especially when the audience has information or views that are as important as your own—it's wise to choose a panel or roundtable discussion rather than a formal presentation or briefing.

Example

As you think about your strategy with HomeCare, you may decide that a preliminary meeting to brief the CEO and officers will be beneficial. The issues that your presentation will address could generate serious conflict or a defensive reaction. An executive briefing may keep the CEO from seeing the report as "us against them" and make him feel an important part of the process.

2. Plan your presentation with the decision maker's main issues in mind.

Put yourself in your audience's position. What does your audience care about? What do they know already? What are their main concerns? In planning your presentation, find the "hot buttons" that will get your audience's attention and engage them in what you are saying. And don't forget to take underlying issues into consideration.

You may have multiple audiences. The recalcitrant CEO may have a CFO or a Human Resources VP who is pushing hard for this project. If so, your presentation must affirm and strengthen the secondary audience's positive attitude without offending the boss.

Example

The CEO of HomeCare doesn't think much of outside consultants. He has been accustomed to running his own show and calling all the shots. You suspect that he has contacted you at someone else's insistence and, quite frankly, because he is desperate. He is still far from convinced that he or his company needs your company's services, but he has some trusted managers who feel strongly that the company needs to make some significant changes.

You also recognize that he is very proprietary about HomeCare Manufacturing Company. It's his "baby," and he doesn't want to lose control. Your strategy must include acknowledging the great job he has done in building the company and finding ways to involve him in the process to fix the problem.

3. Develop a primary message that clearly states what you want to accomplish and why the audience should care about it.

In order to convince your audience, you must know what you want them to do and why they should want to do it. Your primary message should express the common ground between your views and the audience's and act as a benchmark by which you can test every idea. If what you plan to say isn't consistent with this message and pertinent to your argument, discard it or find some other way to present it—possibly in a handout or in leave-behind material.

Example

"You have worked for many years to build a highly successful company that is a leader in its field. For the first time, competitors are beginning to threaten that achievement. High personnel turnover is damaging productivity and profitability. Together we can create an environment that enables your company and its people to realize their full potential."

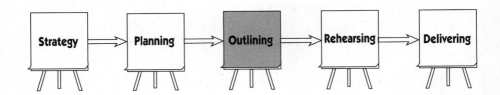

4. Outline your presentation rather than writing it.

Except for press releases and other statements that are designed to be read, you should outline business presentations rather than write them. A script for your presentation is difficult and time consuming to write and will almost certainly produce a stuffy, unnatural effect. And if you write your presentation, you *will* tend to read it—particularly if you get nervous.

In creating your outline, you may find it helpful to use clustering to brainstorm about potential subject matter. Next, use your analysis of the audience to select the points you want to include and the best order for presenting them; then use a presentation planning sheet like the one on page 71 to create a final outline. Transcribe the main points as headings, and list the evidence and examples you want to include under each heading.

In planning, be sure to consider the types of visual support that will be most appropriate to your purpose and the audience. The presentation planning sheet has a separate column for that purpose.

Commentary

It's hard to cross out material that you know well and want to discuss with the audience, but remember that less is more and vice versa. The more topics you discuss, the less the audience will remember about each and the more likely they are to be uncertain which is the most important. Resist the temptation to pile on more and more material. Use your energy instead to find interesting anecdotes and examples to illustrate your main points and good visual material to support your presentation.

If you decide to omit a point that someone may ask about, be prepared (even with supporting visuals) to respond to relevant questions during the question-and-answer session. But during the presentation, tell the audience only what you believe they need to know.

5. Include roadmaps and summaries of important points at major junctures in your presentation.

Every presentation should have an introduction that tells listeners what topics it will cover. It should also have transitions that remind the listeners that they are moving from one point to the next and summarize the major points they have just heard.

After you state your purpose, take a few moments to outline the presentation for the audience, explaining the order and relationship of your topics. As you finish each major section, summarize the

Example

Best Arrangement

Number the topics to indicate the arrangement that makes the most sense to this audience. Then transfer them to the topic outline below. For each major point ask if a visual might help clarify or support your discussion. If so, make a note opposite the point in the column headed "Supporting Visuals."

TOPIC OUTLINE

SUPPORTING VISUALS

HomeCare: A Proud Tradition
- *Point out accomplishments*
- *Emphasize potential for continued success*

What are the issues?
- *High level of attrition*
- *Lost market share*
- *Declining productivity*
- *Low morale, finger pointing*

What's the solution?
- *Team building*
- *Conflict resolution*

main points, remind the audience where they are, and introduce the next section before going on.

Examples

"We've examined the problem. Now let's look at some effective ways to address it and solve it."

"For the next few minutes I want to share with you some success stories of companies who faced similar problems and emerged stronger than ever."

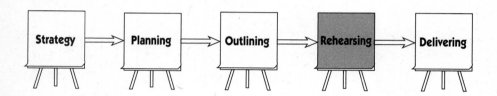

6. Use the majority of your preparation time for rehearsal.

Most speakers mistakenly spend the majority of their preparation time trying to perfect the verbal content of the presentation. Resist the temptation to make elaborate notes and memorize or study them repeatedly. Remember that the words you speak are less than 10 percent of the presentation. If you spend all of your time on words alone, you will be unprepared for 90 percent of the things you must do well when you are standing in front of an audience.

As a general rule, you should spend 25 percent of your preparation time organizing and outlining and 75 percent experimenting with different ways to express your ideas. Some of your rehearsal time can be mental—informally rehearsing individual points in your own mind. But the majority ought to be actual delivery of the material. What looks great on paper may sound hopelessly stiff and awkward coming out of your mouth. Or it may be more than you need to support the point you want to make. You won't know that until you actually try to deliver the presentation you have planned.

Consider also the room setup, the best medium for your visuals, and the seating arrangement. The checklist on pages 75–76 lists items you should consider when planning a presentation.

Commentary

Conversations with friends and associates are excellent rehearsal opportunities—chances for you to get comfortable with expressing your ideas and gauging an audience's reaction to them. For important presentations, rehearse in front of a mirror or other members of your team. Better yet, use a camcorder to videotape the presentation.

As you look at the videotape, try to decide what *one* thing you are doing best, and make a conscious attempt to continue doing it. At the same time, try to identify the one thing that would most improve the delivery. Perhaps you need to rearrange some parts of the presentation or change the way you use your hands or voice. Whatever it turns out to be, concentrate on that alone. If you try to improve everything at once, you won't be able to improve anything enough to make a noticeable difference.

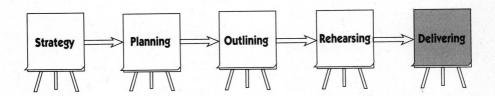

7. Establish a strong connection with the audience.

Eye contact is the single most important element in nonverbal communication and may account for as much as 80 percent of the nonverbal messages we send. Use that information to your advantage by establishing significant eye contact with individual listeners in all parts of the audience. Do not scan the audience or look over their heads to the back of the room. Treat your presentation as if it were a one-on-one conversation with every member of the audience—one person at a time. The individual feedback can be enormously helpful.

Remember, however, that cultural norms differ on eye contact. In some parts of the world, including some parts of the United States, making direct eye contact is rude. Do your homework and know your audience when presenting in an intercultural environment.

Take full advantage of your personal presence by using tone of voice, emphasis, voice level, gestures, and facial expressions to reinforce your message. Remember that the greater the physical distance between you and your audience, the more you will need to exaggerate all of these elements to produce the impact you want.

8. Learn to recognize and rely on nonverbal messages.

Take full advantage of the audience's personal presence by expecting immediate feedback and using it to make the presentation more effective. As you make eye contact, poll the audience for signs that they have understood your point, that you need to move more quickly or more slowly through the material, or that you have missed an important issue that you need to address. Don't be afraid to adjust your remarks to suit their needs or to deviate from your outline if it seems necessary.

These nonverbal messages are yet another good reason not to depend heavily on elaborate notes. If you read from notes or a written text, you lose much of your ability to react to the audience and their concerns.

9. Maintain control of the presentation environment.

Even when you are showing a videotape or someone in the audience is asking a question, you still have the responsibility to be sure the presentation is on track to its objectives. During your final preparation, arrange the room the way you want it, check out all your equipment to make sure that it works properly, and make sure that you know how to operate it. Then stay alert for any potential distractions that can derail the presentation.

PRESENTATION CHECKLIST

While You Plan

☐ Room size. Is it appropriate for the number of participants?

☐ Furniture arrangement. An auditorium setup may be best for a lecture or formal presentation, a horseshoe for training, a square or circle for a meeting or sales presentation. Be sure, too, that you have room to move around easily if you need to do so. Finally, be sure the furniture is comfortable, especially if you plan a long presentation.

☐ Lighting. Will the lighting allow participants to see each other well, take notes, or read handouts? If you plan to darken the room for slides or overheads, can the lights be dimmed? Can you cover the windows?

☐ HVAC system. Is the room temperature controlled by a separate thermostat? Is the system noisy?

☐ Audiovisual support. Do you need a slide projector, overhead projector, projection screen, flip chart(s), monitor/VCR?

☐ Other support requirements. Will you need name badges, cardboard "tent" cards, pads and pencils, a table for handouts? Will you need a microphone and, if so, do you want a portable one?

The Day of the Presentation

Arrive at least 30 minutes in advance to correct anything that isn't arranged according to your plan.

☐ Furniture arrangement. Is the furniture properly arranged?

☐ Lighting. Is the lighting correctly adjusted? If you plan to darken the room for slides or overheads, do you know how to dim the lights and operate the window coverings?

☐ HVAC system. Is the room comfortable? Do you know how to adjust the temperature or who to call if building maintenance must change the thermostat setting?

(continues)

- ☐ Projection equipment. Is the slide projector or overhead in good working order, positioned correctly in the room, and in focus? Does the projector have a spare bulb? Do you know how to operate the equipment?

- ☐ Other support requirements. Is the sound level on the microphone correctly set? Do you know how to adjust it and who to call if the sound system fails to operate correctly? Are the tent cards in place and the materials laid out according to your instructions? Do you have extra copies of handouts?

- ☐ Distractions. Is there a telephone in the room that can ring during the presentation? Are previous presenters' materials on the table or on the walls of the room?

Since Murphy's Law seems to operate with special force during presentations, professional presenters find it helpful to carry an emergency kit just in case. Depending on your anxiety level, you may want to include one or more of the following:

- ☐ Extra bulb for overhead projector
- ☐ Roll of masking tape
- ☐ Marking pens for transparencies, flip charts, dry erase boards, etc.
- ☐ Blank transparency foils
- ☐ Glass cleaner and towels for overhead projector and transparencies
- ☐ Aspirin, antacid, decongestant, and other personal effects, including safety pins, shoeshine materials, an extra pair of pantyhose, a spare pair of glasses, a small pair of scissors, etc.
- ☐ A box of throat lozenges
- ☐ Four flip chart pages (You can tape them together to make a screen in case the room has a patterned or dark-colored wall and the projection screen fails to appear.)
- ☐ An extension cord and a three-prong to two-prong converter

MANAGING VISUALS

The same principles that govern the design of illustrations in written work apply to overheads, slides, and other visual materials you may use in a presentation. To be effective, a visual should be *visual*—it should draw its impact more from graphics and other nonverbal information than from numbers or words. It should also have a single, clear point that is immediately apparent to the audience.

As you prepare the visuals for your presentation, you may find it helpful to review the guidelines for designing visual material in "Designing Visuals." Pay particular attention to the guidelines for making visuals easy to read and understand. Remember that the audience has less time to study a visual in a presentation than in a document. Therefore, your visuals should be simple and easy for the audience to grasp.

1. Incorporate visuals only when you need to emphasize or clarify a point.

Effective presenters use a few strategically placed and well-designed visuals to support their presentations. Unfortunately, the majority of corporate presenters have yet to learn from their example. Most come to the podium armed with a stack of overheads heavy with bullets and text. As a result, their visuals soon lose whatever visual impact they had.

When every point has its own overhead, the audience pays less attention to each point and to the presenter, who quickly fades into the background as a mere "voice-over" to the visual material.

By all means, take advantage of presentation software, which can facilitate preparation and open the door to visual effects that would otherwise be too expensive for most occasions. Remember, however, that even the most sophisticated visuals cannot disguise a poorly designed presentation. Remember, too, that the ease with which you can create visuals with computer software can actually promote "chart junk." Resist the temptation to use graphic overkill, characterized by 3-D effects, vibrating patterns, and extraneous grids, borders, and boxes.

Some rules of thumb:

- Usually, five overheads or slides are plenty for a short presentation. Try to make do with less.
- If you use a text slide or overhead, it should have one central idea and no more than five (but preferably two or three) bulleted, supporting points. It will be significantly more effective if you include a well-done drawing to illustrate the central idea.

2. Design visuals with the audience and room size in mind.

Visuals that support presentations should always be visible as well as visual. Don't assume that because the titles and drawings look great on the artist's drawing table they will look good on a screen. Graphics should be clear even from the back of the room. Make sure titles and other print are at least 18 point (1/4" high) for small and medium sized rooms, 36 point (1/2" high) for larger settings.

Example

This is 12 point type. It's fine for documents but too small for overheads.

This is 18 point.

This is 36 point.

Commentary

Never use an entire page of text, an entire income statement, or an entire spreadsheet as a visual. Not only are the numbers or words too small for the audience to read comfortably, but the visual also lacks a focal point and you will confuse the audience or lose their attention. Select the numbers or the relationships you want the audience to remember and display them prominently, either in a miniature table or in a graph that clarifies their relationship and significance.

Examples

Ineffective Visual:

Breakdown of Operating Expenses
Fiscal Year 1994 (Projected)

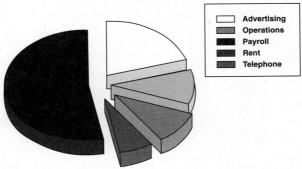

- Three-dimensional, tilted effect distorts relationships among the slices.
- Title fails to indicate what is important in the visual.
- Legend forces viewer to match patterns to identify slices.
- Explosion and shading of slices lacks clear relationship to message.

Effective Visual:

Payroll Will Be More Than 50% of 1994 Operating Expenses.

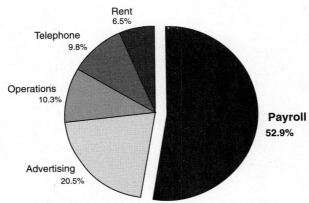

- Two-dimensional chart more accurately represents relationships among the slices.
- Title summarizes the visual message and controls viewer expecations.
- Explosion, shading, and position (at 12 o'clock) of "Payroll" slice contribute to the visual message.
- Each slice is clearly labeled with its name and percentage value.

Ineffective Visual:

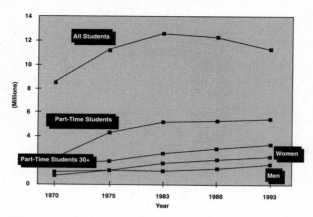

- Graph contains too much information.
- Title is too general.
- Data lines float in space and away from the vertical axis.

Effective Visual:

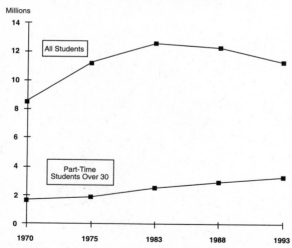

- Graph has a single clear point, with a heavy line for the most important variable.
- Vertical axis anchors data lines.
- Title summarizes the visual message and controls interpretation.
- Reduced clutter clarifies relationship between variables.

3. Maintain your rapport with the audience while using the visual.

Even while a visual is on the screen, you are still responsible for making sure that the audience sees what you want them to see and that they see it as your point. Otherwise, you will have to reestablish rapport with the audience when you have finished with the visual and are ready to move on.

Some ways to maintain rapport:

■ Introduce the visual in a way that will help the audience see what point it makes and how it fits into what you have been saying.

Example

"Our competitor's new sports car has had a dramatic impact on our sales. Here's what has happened since February, when they introduced it."

■ Wait to turn the projector on until you are ready for the audience to see the visual. Turn the projector off when you have finished making your point and the audience has understood it.

■ If you are using a slide projector, turn it off between slides or insert black slides between the visual materials so the screen will be dark until you are ready to talk about the next visual.

■ Interact with the visual, but always speak to the audience. If you point to something in the visual, find what you want to point to, put your finger or the pointer on it, then turn and address your comments to the audience. The same advice applies to flip charts, mockups, and other types of visuals. *Whenever you are talking, you should have eye contact with someone in the audience.*

■ When you use an overhead projector, interact with the projected image, not the projector. Placing pencils and other pointing devices on the projection surface distracts the audience from the projected image; it puts you between them and the image; and it shines light up into your face so you can't see them. You can ignore this guideline during an informal presentation when you are using the overhead projector as you would a flip chart and writing on a sheet of transparency paper with a marker.

- If possible, leave the lights on when you are showing slides or overhead transparencies. The image will still be visible and so will you. You can't maintain good rapport with the audience if you are both in the dark.

- Wait until the presentation is over to hand out photocopies and other supporting materials. It's a good idea to furnish materials that the audience can use to review important points. It's not a good idea to have them rustling papers, paging ahead, or worst of all, asking questions about the table on page 37 that you didn't want to discuss at all.

- If you show a text visual with more than one statement, run through all of the statements quickly to set the agenda before discussing any of them in detail. Use a separate visual as you expand on each statement. That way, the audience will stay with you instead of wandering ahead to speculate about what is next and how it might fit with the point you are now making.

- Controlling the audience's perception of the visual doesn't mean standing in front of the screen. Be sure that everyone has an unobstructed view of the visual. Point with the hand closest to the image. If you are using overhead transparencies, move back away from the overhead projector after you turn it on so that those in the front and off to the side can see clearly.

HANDLING QUESTIONS AND ANSWERS

Many presenters dread throwing the floor open to questions for fear of losing control of the presentation or being asked a question they aren't prepared to answer. In reality, the question-and-answer session can be a valuable tool for engaging the audience and driving home the presentation's message. Good presenters welcome questions, but they maintain command of the situation by handling the process effectively.

Most questioners will want you to elaborate on points you made during the presentation. In such cases, you can use the opportunity to provide additional evidence for your overall thesis. Others, however, may raise concerns or issues that you didn't address or even anticipate. And still others may ask questions that are intended to undermine or distract you from your overall objective. To be effective, you must be able to deal with all types of questions and questioners. Here are some guidelines to enhance your effectiveness and the impact of your presentation.

1. Tell your audience whether you will handle questions during the presentation or at the end.

Some presenters encourage the audience to ask questions during the presentation; others ask them to wait until the end. Either is acceptable.

Leaving yourself open to questions during the presentation usually works best when you are presenting complex or technical information and you want to keep the audience from getting lost or confused. It also works well when you are dealing with unexplored or emotional issues—ones where the audience may need to participate and be acknowledged.

It is generally best to ask the audience to hold their questions until the end if you plan to deliver a formal, highly structured presentation and must work within specified time limits.

Saving questions and answers until the end of the presentation can be anticlimactic if the audience has no questions or their questions are inconsequential or beside the point. One way to avoid this problem is to save your concluding remarks until after the audience has finished asking questions.

Example

"If you don't have further questions, let me quickly summarize the main points that we discussed here today...."

Commentary

When you take questions during the session, the presentation can assume many of the characteristics of a meeting. Under such circumstances, you should draw upon the techniques for effective meeting management. For example, use the presentation overview as an agenda to help make sure that the group stays on track and the questions don't get too far afield. After discussing a question, summarize the discussion, then redirect the audience's attention to the agenda.

2. Ask for questions in a way that encourages the audience to respond.

Sometimes members of the audience are reluctant to be the first to ask a question. After all, asking a question suddenly puts them on stage. Give the audience a chance to gather up their courage. When you're standing alone in front of a group, 20 or 30 seconds can seem like an eternity, but discipline yourself to wait for questioners to collect their thoughts.

3. Create a low-risk environment for your audience.

Treat every question and questioner with respect. Except for overt harassment, never show impatience with a question. Be sure the audience knows that you value their response and that you won't embarrass or attack them if they ask a question.

Commentary

If members of the audience are apprehensive about your reaction to their questions, they may be reluctant to participate. You may want to relax the audience a bit by asking them some questions and encouraging them to answer, either with a show of hands or by speaking up. This technique will get them accustomed to the question-and-answer format and will make them feel more confident about speaking up.

4. Listen carefully to the question, and make sure that everyone else heard and understood it.

Give questioners your undivided attention while they are speaking. And be sure you let them finish their question before you begin to speak.

When you are speaking to a large group, repeat the question for the entire audience to hear. Often questioners are either shy about speaking up and ask their questions too quietly, or they have their backs turned to a large part of the audience.

Commentary

Too often speakers think they understand the question and begin to answer before the questioner is finished. Resist the temptation to jump in with an answer.

Don't lapse into a stock comment on the question, either, with responses such as "That's a very good question," or, "I'm glad you asked that." The next questioner might wonder why you aren't glad he or she asked a particular question. On the other hand, it's fine to mention that someone has made a point that contributes to understanding the subject. And if someone raises an issue that you forgot to mention, admit it, respond as best you can, and thank the participant for the contribution.

Avoid calling the questioner by name unless you know everyone's name in the group. Those you don't know may feel excluded. If you know one or two participants particu-

(continues)

larly well, however, it's fine to say something like, "Bob, I'm sure you're thinking of the Morris project, when a similar set of circumstances caused the situation that you are asking about."

5. Use eye contact to keep the entire group involved.

Make eye contact with the questioner while he or she is asking the question and as you begin to answer. Then, as you continue, reestablish eye contact with other members of the group. As you finish answering the question, return to the questioner and make strong eye contact to close out the response.

6. If you don't know the answer, say so.

Never try to bluff your way through a question-and-answer session. If you don't know the answer, say "I'm sorry. I don't know, but I'll find out and get back to you," and follow through on your promise. Or you may throw the question out to the group: "I don't know. Can anyone else help us?"

7. Keep your answers short.

Your audience has already sat through one presentation. Don't make them suspect you're getting your second wind and are going to deliver another. Keep your answers short and to the point.

Commentary

If the questioner still seems unsatisfied, ask, "Does that answer your question?" If a full answer will take longer, offer to discuss the question afterwards.

Don't let yourself be pulled into a dialogue with a single questioner. If you answer one question and the questioner immediately asks another, tell that person that you need to answer the questions of others and that you will come back to him or her later.

USING THE TELEPHONE EFFECTIVELY

Talking on the telephone requires a somewhat different approach from talking face to face. When we talk on the telephone, the communication channel narrows drastically. We no longer have access to body language, facial expressions, eye contact, and other important visual clues that tell what the listener is thinking or feeling. Nor can we use these resources ourselves to communicate our ideas.

Even in the midst of increasingly sophisticated office automation, the telephone remains one of the most important pieces of office technology. Business couldn't run without it. Yet no business tool frustrates quite as much as the telephone. We play endless rounds of telephone tag, and we lose productivity every day, being put on hold, getting busy signals, or placing calls that don't reach the intended receiver. When we *do* get an answer, we frequently spend too much time in idle chit-chat, wasting our own time and the other person's as well.

On the positive side, effective telephone communication can have a significant impact on both our personal effectiveness and the image we project of ourselves and the organization we represent. Nor are there many new skills to learn. Effective telephone skills incorporate many of the same techniques that you need to lead or participate in a meeting, make a presentation, or conduct an interview.

1. Establish your objectives before you make the call.

The secret to using the telephone effectively is planning. Have an agenda, and know exactly what you hope to accomplish. Remember that, as the caller, you are responsible for guiding the conversation and making sure that it achieves its objectives.

Example

You are a computer software salesperson calling the information systems director at a large trucking company. You want an appointment to demonstrate the features of your software, but the IS director keeps trying to steer the conversation toward price. If you keep your objective in mind, you can avoid being drawn into a discussion of price by assuring her that you will cover all relevant information and details in your meeting. Your objective is to get an appointment, not to sell software over the telephone.

Commentary

Jot down the main points you want to make on a pad so you won't forget anything important. Then take notes during the conversation so that you can keep a record of the call and follow up on the telephone meeting with specific action.

2. Put energy and expression into your voice.

Your voice becomes your personality on the telephone. Sit up in your chair; use facial expressions and gestures as you would if you were speaking face to face.

Instead of putting less into a telephone conversation than into a face-to-face encounter, we actually need to *increase* our vocal effectiveness to compensate for what we have lost in nonverbal communication.

Try taping your end of a telephone conversation and listening to it after you hang up. You may be surprised to hear how you come across when all you have to go on is your voice.

For the same reasons, maintaining control on the telephone is more difficult than in a face-to-face conversation. You can't keep visitors from interrupting or distracting your listener. Neither can you keep him or her from reading mail or typing on the computer. You must compensate for this disadvantage by making your conversation lively, relevant, and interesting.

3. Speak clearly and at a rate people can understand.

Articulate carefully. Although telephones reproduce the human voice well, you need to speak more clearly than you do in person.

As in any oral presentation, speak slowly enough (100–120 words per minute) and leave enough pauses that the other person has time to absorb what you are saying.

Speak in an ordinary conversational tone, but raise your voice slightly when you need to emphasize a point.

4. Listen more than you talk.

Listen harder than you would in person. Because the feedback loop is limited without the visual components of the conversation, you must be more alert for whatever cues you can pick up. Use effective listening techniques such as

- Questions.
- Encouraging signals, such as "Yes," "I see," "Uh-huh."
- Listening checks: "If your schedule is that tight, then you need this information by tomorrow morning."
- Open-ended comments: "That's interesting. Tell me how the program will apply to new employees."

5. Begin your call effectively.

Identify yourself immediately and pleasantly. Don't make your caller try to figure out who you are. Begin with a courteous greeting to establish rapport, and state your business immediately. Otherwise, you may fail to get your listener's attention and waste valuable time.

Example

Caller's Words	Listener's Mental Reaction
Hi, this is Ted.	(Ted who?)
I called to get those sales figures.	(What figures?)
After we talked at the quarterly meeting, I decided to use that format you suggested.	(What meeting? What format? Who is this guy?)
(Sensing some confusion) I'm in corporate planning. I wanted to get last year's sales totals, by region.	(Of course. Why didn't he say so at first?)
Can you help me?	Sure, I can get them to you. Tell me your name again.

6. End your call effectively.

End your call when you have accomplished your objective. Don't allow yourself to be drawn into nonproductive conversation.

Since you placed the call, you can end it. Thank the person for his or her time and for the information. You may also refer to some future contact.

Examples

"I'll call you tomorrow and tell you how the meeting went."

"I've got to go now because I have an appointment in five minutes. Thanks for your help. I'll check back with you on Friday to see how the report is coming along."

"This has been a big help. Thank you for your time. Have a good weekend."

7. When someone calls you, answer the telephone courteously and professionally.

Identify yourself and, in some cases, your position or department.

Examples

"Billing Department. Jane Smith."

"Crocker's Restaurant. This is Thomas Crocker. May I help you?"

"This is Marcus Price. How can I help you?"

Give the caller your full attention. Don't type on the computer, read your mail, or try to carry on a conversation in hand signals with someone in your office. People can tell when you are distracted or only half listening.

8. Minimize delays.

Everyone hates to be put on hold, and unnecessary delays can undermine your relationship with the caller. If the caller has to wait for you to come on the line, apologize. If you have to look for information before you can continue the conversation, offer to call the person back immediately rather than have him or her wait on the line.

Never have a secretary place a call for you and put the person on hold until you pick up the telephone. The message you send to the other person is "My time is more important than yours."

9. Return *all* your telephone calls promptly or have an appropriate person do so.

Enhance your professional image by returning all telephone calls as quickly as possible, even if you don't want to talk to the person. No one should have to leave multiple messages without speaking with you. If the caller is out when you call back, be sure to leave a message that you returned the call. But don't let the situation degenerate into telephone tag. Suggest some times when you will be in your office and available to talk. Or ask when the person will be available to talk and set up an appointment to call back.

Example

"Please tell Mr. Morris I'll call tomorrow morning between 10:00 and 10:30."

If the person has requested information that someone else can provide, pass the message on but follow up to make sure that the third party made the call.

10. Use a speaker phone only when necessary.

Use a speaker phone *only* when more than one person on your end must participate in the conversation or when the call requires your hands to be free—for example, if you must operate a computer keyboard to obtain information that the caller needs.

Speaker phones call attention to the elements missing in the communication channel and suggest that the person using it may be doing other things or someone else may be listening in.

They also magnify background noise and impair the intimacy of the conversation.

11. Treat message machines and voice mail more like memos than conversations.

When using voice mail systems, plan your message carefully. As in all communication, answer the questions, "What's new?", "Why should I care?", and "What do you want me to do about it?" Send your message concisely and clearly, using the same guidelines you would in a memo.

Example

Memo Element	Voice Mail Message
To:	Hi, George.
From:	This is Marsha Baker.
Date:	It's 3:25 on Monday afternoon. (*Not necessary if the voice mail system has a date/time stamp.*)
Subject:	I wanted to bring you up to date on this morning's budget meeting so that you'll be ready for your session with Dave tomorrow.

A voice mail system or answering machine narrows the communication channel even further than an ordinary telephone call. Not only have you lost visual cues, but you have also lost the verbal feedback you normally get in a telephone conversation. For this reason, people tend to talk too much, as if waiting for the nonexistent person on the other end to respond. Keep your message short. If you think it's going on too long, it probably is.

If you have a personal message machine or voice mailbox in your office, change your message frequently. Not only will callers appreciate the more personal touch, but you can also let them know when you will be available to talk.

Example

"This is Joe Bernardo. Today is Thursday, February 25. I'm out of the office all day at a meeting but will be back in on Friday, February 26. I'll return your call no later than noon tomorrow."

Commentary

Only about 25 percent of all business calls reach their intended recipient on the first try. As a result, managers and staff spend 30 minutes a day, or almost 13 days a year, on hold, getting a busy signal or no answer, and playing telephone tag.

When you simply need to convey information and don't have to talk to the person you are calling, voice mail systems are effective and offer the following additional advantages:

- More message security than handwritten notes. (But don't assume total privacy. Although most voice mail systems are password protected, the information they contain is still vulnerable to some extent.)

- Accuracy and reliability. You leave your own message, so there is no risk of transcription errors or other third-party foul-ups.

- Efficiency. No needless chit-chat, and you can send messages to a number of people with one telephone call.

Commentary

A NOTE ABOUT MOBILE PHONES

Mobile telephones, once considered frivolous, have become an integral part of the way we do business. Used wisely, they provide convenience, security, and efficiency.

(continues)

Generally, mobile telephones aren't suited for extended conversation unless your time is so valuable that you can't afford the dead time that you spend in the car. When you are talking and driving, you can't take notes or look at papers. They're great, however, for calling a client to say that you're running late or to ask for directions should you get lost on the way.

The distraction can be a safety hazard. Any time you take your eyes off the road, even to dial, you're asking for trouble. In fact, some states now require hands-free attachments to prevent people from holding the handset while driving. If your telephone has a speed-dial feature, use it to program frequently called numbers.

In addition to the cost and safety factors, varying signal strength within an area can result in irritating static or a broken connection.

To get the most benefits from your mobile telephone, plan what you're going to say. Treat mobile telephone calls like voice mail. Remember that less is more. Identify your objectives, organize your message, and, in most cases, aim for brevity.

PART FOUR

WORKING IN GROUPS

We seem to have the most at stake when we stand alone in front of an audience or send an important memo. But now more than ever careers depend on how well business people work with others, individually or in groups.

Today, organizations need managers with highly developed interpersonal communication skills. Listening, probing for different points of view, waiting to hear several sides of the issue on hard-to-solve problems—all are necessary for participative management to work and for employees to take ownership of work objectives.

We have designed the guidelines in the following sections to help you manage group efforts more effectively. We begin with guidelines for managing a meeting; then we present an approach to group writing projects that seems to work better than the usual methods. Finally, we offer a few guidelines for planning and delivering group presentations, a common phenomenon not only in academic settings but also in advertising, consulting, and other professional services.

MANAGING A MEETING

With increased emphasis on teams and matrix management, the ability to work productively in groups has assumed critical importance. More reputations are made on the way managers conduct themselves in meetings, in one-to-one discussions with other decision makers, and in performance reviews and briefing sessions than in any other way.

Disappointingly, managers estimate that more than one-third of the time they spend in meetings is wasted—with near-disastrous results for themselves and their firms. The following guidelines will help steer you past mistakes even experienced managers make when they gather to make a decision.

1. Be sure you need to hold a meeting.

You need to hold a meeting if

- You and your group must make a decision or diagnose a problem that requires more skills, information, or time than any one person can contribute.
- The issue has more than one acceptable solution or decision, and each has its advocates.
- The personal presence of the members or the leader is essential for social, political, or motivational reasons.

2. Know whose meeting it is.

For a meeting to achieve its objectives, someone must plan the meeting, prepare an agenda, and make sure that everyone gets an opportunity to participate. If you called the meeting, or are managing it, you are responsible for its success. You waste everyone's time and damage your credibility if the meeting misses its objectives because you let it get out of control.

In emergencies or other situations in which no one has taken responsibility for the meeting, deciding who will manage it should be the first order of business.

3. Take time to plan.

- Round up relevant papers and data, or make sure that someone else does.

- Sound out potential participants to preview their ideas and identify their concerns.

- Anticipate problems and issues, and discover how they are related.

4. Write an agenda, and distribute it two to three days in advance.

This is the most critical step in preparing for the meeting. A good agenda should contain

- The day, date, time, and place of the meeting.

  Show both the starting and ending times for the meeting. Remember that meetings longer than 90 minutes are highly unproductive; to maximize the value of the participants' time, schedule the meeting to last an hour or less.

- The names of those who will attend, including their titles and/or departments.

  For meetings that involve problem solving or decision making, 4 to 7 participants is best. Any more than 10 is crowd control.

  If the list of participants is too large, check to see if some agenda items can be decided in preliminary mini-meetings. Also be sure that every participant on the list must be present for the entire meeting. (Generally, a person should attend the whole of a meeting only if he or she has significant input for two-thirds of the agenda items.)

- The meeting objective(s), including specific outcomes expected from the meeting.

  Generalized, vague objectives ("Review sales forecast") do little to help participants prepare for the meeting. To be useful, descriptions of objectives and outcomes must be specific and results oriented ("Review and approve increases for European distributors in third quarter sales forecast.")

- A list of agenda items or topics in the order they will be discussed.

  In addition to specific, results-oriented descriptions of the items, consider allocating amounts of time for each. Doing so not only

Sample Agenda

MEETING AGENDA

DATE: July 18, 199X

TO: Joyce Bergman   Dick Rodriguez
                Product Manager   Product Manager
                Personal Communication   Personal Communication
                  Systems   Systems

                Lisa Carroll   Jim Thompkins
                Sr. Project Engineer   Market Research

                Robert Colegrove   John LaBout
                Senior Planner   Manager, European
                Manufacturing Operations   Sales (By telephone)

FROM: George Gansser
                General Manager
                Personal Communication Systems

SUBJECT: MONTHLY SALES FORECAST MEETING

This is to request or confirm your attendance at the following meeting:

DATE(S): July 29, 199X   **TIME:** 7:00 a.m. - 8:00 a.m.
PLACE: Meeting Room A, Lakeview Center

MEETING OBJECTIVE: Review and approve increases for European distributors in Q4

ITEMS TO BE DISCUSSED	TIME IN MINUTES
Introductions and Overview of Agenda (George Gansser)	5

Review European Marketplace Trends (Jim Thompkins)
    Sales figures for the past six quarters are attached.
    Please review them before the meeting.
	10

Approve Revised Forecast for Personal Telephones
    Size of increase
    Distribution of additional sales
    Distributor sales force requirements
    Other issues
	20

Approve Revised Pager Forecast
    Size of increase
    Distribution of additional sales
    Pricing for EC distributors
    Other issues
	15

Wrapup and Review of Action Items	10

indicates the relative importance of each item to participants, but also helps serve as a reality check for you.

Commentary

If you have given out assignments in advance or attached documents for participants to read, it's a good idea to note them after the appropriate item. ("Jim Thompkins will discuss briefly the major trends in the European marketplace. Please take time before the meeting to look at the breakdown of sales for the past six quarters.") Even when you don't make specific assignments, highlight items of special significance and give some background information to help participants start thinking about the problem they will need to address.

The logical flow of the meeting is critical. The arrangement of items must bring order to the discussion and make sense to the participants. A frequently used series of steps for problem-solving meetings begins with a statement of the problem and ends with action steps to implement the decision the group has reached:

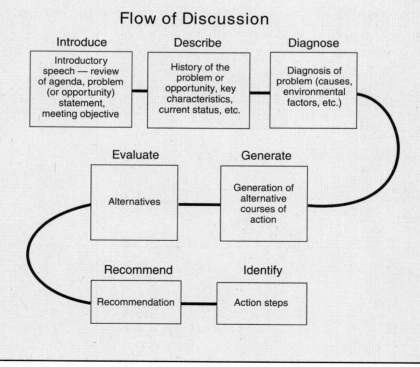

Flow of Discussion

Introduce	Describe	Diagnose
Introductory speech — review of agenda, problem (or opportunity) statement, meeting objective	History of the problem or opportunity, key characteristics, current status, etc.	Diagnosis of problem (causes, environmental factors, etc.)

Evaluate	Generate
Alternatives	Generation of alternative courses of action

Recommend	Identify
Recommendation	Action steps

5. Open the meeting with an effective introductory speech.

- Take one or two minutes (not more) to review the background of the problem, the meeting objective(s), and expected outcomes. Preview the projected problem-solving process, including the role of key players. Make sure your introduction is action and results oriented. The more concise and businesslike your opening statement, the more businesslike the meeting will be.

- After your introductory speech, get a verbal and visual agreement on the agenda from all participants. Now is the time to deal with misunderstandings and hidden agendas, not later.

Commentary

If you are a participant and the leader has not done a good job to this point, don't sign off until you are satisfied that everything is in order. ("George, I'm confused. Shouldn't we review the changes in pricing before we look at the new forecast?")

6. Keep the discussion on target.

- Remind the group of the time limits on each item. As they pass important milestones in the agenda, help them measure progress and keep track of where they are by announcing the time and summarizing results.

- Cut off discussions that are not clearly related to the meeting objectives. In doing so, avoid bruising tender egos. Acknowledge the value of individual comments, and promise to deal with good but marginally relevant ideas later. Be specific about the uses for the idea and what "later" means; follow up after the meeting if you value your credibility.

Example

"John, that's an excellent idea for reformatting the forecast. I'll mention it to Fred Carr in market research right after the meeting."

Commentary

Other ways to deal with wayward discussions:

- Summarize progress and redirect discussion to the item at hand: "From what everyone has said so far, it sounds as if we agree about the effect the new pricing will have. Unless someone has something different to add, let's move on to the forecast itself."

- Challenge the relevance of the topic: "Maybe I don't understand your point, Bob, but I can't see how GE's experience will help us with the decision we have to make today."

- Use posture, eye contact, facial expression, and gestures to close a topic and shift the discussion to other participants.

7. Always strive to be a servant of the group rather than its master.

Effective groups recognize and draw on the energy inherent in difference without being overcome by conflict. This means that, as leader, you must

- Draw out reluctant members of the group, especially those who may be hostile to an idea the group favors or timid souls in possession of a good idea they are afraid may be rejected.

- Call attention to apparent discrepancies and misunderstandings, emerging problems, and underlying assumptions.

- Support the integrity of the group by

  - Protecting the weak.

  - Highlighting the hidden value in apparently worthless ideas.

  - Defusing critical attacks, especially personal ones.

  - Helping the group build constructive, high-quality solutions by making connections between one idea and another and asking for responses to useful suggestions.

- Ask more questions than you answer—and ask them well. A good question is brief, relevant, simply worded, and directed to a single point. One manager restricts her interventions in group discussions to one sentence. Allow yourself two, if they are both short; but consider it a danger signal if you hear yourself talking at length between your introduction and your summary of the meeting's achievements.

- Stay out of conflicts. Most researchers agree that the leader of the meeting must keep his or her "social leadership" even if it means sacrificing "task leadership." To put it another way, the leader must serve the common interest of the group even if it means seeing his or her favorite idea go down in flames. The reason is simple: If the leader is seen as an advocate for a particular point of view, it significantly decreases—perhaps even destroys—his or her ability to resolve conflicts between differing factions.

Commentary

If you are a participant, you can contribute by doing the same things as the leader:

- Creating opportunities for others to speak.

- Questioning the validity of your own assumptions and opinions.

- Expressing your reservations about others' ideas in a direct and specific but nonthreatening way.

- Considering the value of others' ideas and opinions carefully before pressing for your own.

Just as the best leaders are good followers, the best followers usually help the leader where they can by taking the group's interests to heart and some of the weight off the leader's shoulders.

8. Learn to recognize and rely on nonverbal messages.

Whether you are the leader or a participant, keep strong eye contact with all members of the group. Use gestures, facial expressions, and variations in the pitch, rate, and volume of your voice to add energy and authority to your ideas. When you are speaking—and even when you are not—watch for nonverbal signs of understanding and agreement (smiles, nods) or disagreement (averted eyes, changes in posture, tapping fingers, etc.).

9. End the meeting on a positive note.

- Close the meeting when any of the following occurs:
    - Time runs out.
    - You have finished the agenda.
    - You are without someone or something you must have in order to continue.

- Close the meeting by
    - Summarizing accomplishments.
    - Thanking the participants for their time and contributions (the more specific and personal your praise, the better).
    - Reviewing the list of action items that have accumulated during the meeting. Be sure that each action item includes a due date and the name of the participant who accepted responsibility for it.

MANAGING GROUP WRITING PROJECTS

If you have read "Managing a Meeting" and "Managing the Writing Process," you will find little here that is new. If you study the chart that follows, you will see that we have simply assigned the steps in the writing process to the resources that can handle them most effectively.

Step 1. Planning I

Group

- Select topic.
- Define objective(s), audience(s), scope.
- Develop list of key questions and issues.
- Brainstorm resources.
- Define roles and assignments.
  - Project management
  - Research
  - Writing
  - Graphics production
- Set schedule with deadlines.

Step 2. Planning II

Research

- Deliver short (5- to 10-minute) presentation on findings.

Group

- Develop overall plan/topic outline. Show development, major points, important evidence/data, preliminary ideas about illustrations and graphics.
- Compile "To Get" list of additional information, illustration material, etc.

Research

- Deliver information packets to writer(s).

Step 3. Drafting

Writer(s)

- Complete rough draft with preliminary illustration material or sketches with descriptions of material required. Headings and subheadings should be in place.

Step 4. Rough Editing

Group

- Compare draft to plan.
- Examine development, selection, and arrangement of material, appropriateness of graphics.
- Suggest revisions, especially enhancements to development of ideas (no revisions at sentence level during this session).

Writer

- Incorporate changes.

Step 5. Fine Editing and Proofreading

Writer/Editor/Project Manager

- Edit at sentence level.
- Assemble document.
- Proofread and submit (no substantive changes at this stage).

1. **Meet as a group to set objectives and define roles.**

    Steps 1 and 2, strategy and planning, are work for the group. The synergies that come from many heads working together almost always create more ideas than individuals can—as long as the group works together effectively.

2. **Choose your best writer to draft the document and perform the final editing.**

    Steps 3 and 5, drafting and fine editing the document, are best done by one person who writes well and quickly. If you have ever been part of a group that tried to fine edit a document together, you will know why.

3. **Use the rough editing step as an opportunity for the group to assess the draft in relation to the plan and make substantive revisions.**

    Step 4, rough editing, is work for the group again, since all members of the group should want to compare the structure and content of the document to the plan they developed in Steps 1 and 2 and to suggest improvements.

Commentary

Unfortunately, most groups do not work together as effectively as they might. Instead, they forget to plan, manage their time together badly, and put off important decisions about emphasis and structure until they finish the first draft. And they often insist that each member write a section of the document, even when they have not fully discussed how the sections should fit together. No wonder that when they all meet to consider the first draft, each with a separate piece of the puzzle, the finished product looks like Frankenstein's monster and the poor "editor" is left to stitch the pieces back together or simply write it from scratch.

(continues)

The next time you tackle a group writing project, try a different approach. Use the group where it can make the biggest impact on the finished result—in planning, brainstorming, and generating and testing ideas and approaches to the problem. Plan carefully how the various ideas fit together, and then leave it to the best writer in the group to present the group's best thinking.

MAKING GROUP PRESENTATIONS

Team presentations are appropriate when members of the audience need to see those with whom they will have continuing contact. For that reason, advertising agencies, consulting groups, and other professional service firms often include key members of their project teams in presentations. Similarly, at the end of a long project, group presentations provide an attractive opportunity for everyone to appear before management and be recognized for individual contributions.

1. Recognize the difficulties of presenting as a team.

Team presentations pose some tough problems. Too often, each presenter develops his or her segment of the presentation without sufficient attention to the whole. As a result, the presentation lacks clear links between one section and another.

In addition, particularly when the presentation lasts 20 minutes or less, the overall effect of introducing more than one presenter can be herky-jerky and confusing to the audience. The audience isn't sure who is in charge, and the message can become blurred as the audience adjusts to each new presenter's idiosyncrasies of dress, voice, or delivery.

For a group presentation to be successful, the participants must carefully orchestrate the process from concept through delivery. As with group writing projects, the synergies of group work can be more powerful than the impact of a single presenter. But the potential for disaster and the need for coordination mean that group presentations are more difficult and more, not less, time consuming to manage than individual ones.

Your initial team meeting should concentrate first on objectives, audience, and strategy, and then on individual roles and assignments. Make sure that everyone has the same concept of the presentation's subject and purpose. Identify topics that will have the most appeal for the audience, and cut away inessential material. Begin to think together about the best way to communicate key ideas visually, with overheads, slides, and demonstrations. Then make assignments for each of the team members based on an outline that the group has developed for the presentation.

2. Choose your best speakers to present.

In group as in individual presentations, the speaker is as important as the message. A fumbling, nervous presenter will make the audience uncomfortable and detract from the power of the message. Remember, not everyone has to speak. Some members of the team can contribute more effectively by doing research, designing and or producing visuals, or just brainstorming with the team about the best way to organize and present the group's ideas.

Commentary

At school, instructors often ask everyone in the group to present in order to be sure they have done their fair share of the work. Generally, we think this is unwise and poor preparation for superior performance on the job. Unless one member wants to take part in the presentation for developmental reasons and the other members of the group agree, choose your best speakers to handle the presentation. If necessary, other members of the group can show that they know the material by participating in the question-and-answer session afterwards. We recommend no more than two presenters for presentations up to an hour in length.

3. Rehearse for the presentation.

Because the continuity of a group presentation depends heavily on prior understandings about each presenter's role and subject matter, rehearsal is far more important than it is for an individual presentation. Plan for at least one rehearsal in which you run through the entire presentation, preferably in the room where you will be presenting. If the final visuals aren't ready, use provisional ones, but practice using them and interacting with them. Don't forget to give members a chance to comment on the effectiveness of the visuals and the organization of the presentation as a whole. Remember, this is the group's opportunity to critique the presentation as well as to rehearse it.

But make sure that you dress rehearse the actual presentation. Too often, members of the group merely talk through what they plan to say. As a result, they are unprepared when they actually step before an audience—and not surprisingly, since they may have rehearsed less than 30 percent of what they need to do.

4. Spend extra time on transitions.

The first speaker should provide a short overview of the presentation and the material each presenter will discuss. This is also a good time to recognize members of the group who have contributed to the project but will not actively participate.

Each presenter, as he or she finishes a segment of the presentation, should summarize briefly and introduce the next presenter's portion as it relates to what has gone before.

Example

"I hope this helps you see the internal difficulties that led the steel industry down the road to bankruptcy in the late '60s. Next, John will discuss the industry's attempts to regain profitability in the face of foreign competition."

Commentary

Always make a clean break between presenters. Pause while you clean up stray papers or, if you are the next speaker, while you set up the materials you need and arrange the presenting area. Too often, presenters talk through their entrances and exits about stage business and other matters unrelated to the presentation. This makes it more difficult to refocus the audience when you are ready to begin. As each new presenter steps into the spotlight, it's a good idea to provide a transition for the audience and an overview of the material he or she will cover.

Example

"As Jill has explained, inadequate capitalization and poor human resource management hurt our industry in the '60s. Now I want to review the steps we took in the '70s to address these problems and how they led to the crisis of the '80s."

5. Monitor each speaker's time during the presentation, and stick to your plan.

Even professional presenters get carried away with their subject and run beyond their allotted time, particularly if the audience is still interested and the presentation is on target. But the group should never allow one segment of the presentation to overbalance the others. Time each segment, and signal when time is up so the presenter can draw to a close. If the presenter doesn't respond, walk on stage and interrupt if necessary to keep things on schedule.

COMMUNICATING IN A CHANGING WORLD

Recent developments in communication technology have forced most knowledge workers, employees and managers alike, to reinvent their communication behavior with each new technological advance. Those who have finally learned to be comfortable speaking to message machines, and can use them to improve the flow and quality of information, must now discover the best way to leverage the capabilities of computer graphics and teleconferencing. And tomorrow they will need to adapt to the specific requirements of picture phones and multimedia presentations.

But there is hope. As emerging technology continues to provide both opportunities and challenges, the principles that we have introduced to manage the communication process still apply. As you experiment with new ways to exchange information, deliver a message, or persuade, you still need to identify your objectives, analyze your audience, and find the common ground where your objectives intersect.

For example, as you use a mobile telephone, participate in a teleconference, or communicate via E-mail or fax, ask yourself:

- Will the audience on the other end of a mobile phone conversation appreciate your efficiency, or will that person consider you trendy or extravagant because you have a car phone? Also, is the subject too sensitive or full of conflict to endure the irritation of static and dropped calls?

- Have you taken as much time to make the information in an E-mail or fax transmission as accessible to busy readers as you would if it were a hard copy document? If your audience is rushed, isn't accessibility more, not less, important?

- Does your message in a teleconference fit the medium? Teleconferences that discuss facts, ideas, or schedules or engage in problem solving are generally more successful than those that negotiate, bargain, or resolve conflict. People tend to be less comfortable dealing with emotion or conflict without the benefit of the many nonverbal cues available in face-to-face conversation.

- Have you considered specifically how your communication practices respond to the demands of a global economy? Clear, concise prose, simple visuals, and documents designed to make information accessible to the reader will become particularly important as we continue to communicate internationally.

In short, we need to remember that new technology is always a double-edged sword. The same technology that makes it possible for managers to communicate with anyone, at any place, at any time, and in any form also adds to the already staggering amount of information that confronts each of us daily. Those who suffer from hyperconnectivity and information anxiety will agree that, for businesses as well as individual managers, the key to progress is not merely access to more technology but the developed ability to use it well. Managers would be wise, then, to stay highly flexible in their approach to communication tasks and to analyze communication strategy until it becomes second nature.

Whatever the future holds, high quality communication will continue to be critical to our success both as individuals and organizations and a challenge to managers at all levels. We hope that this book helps meet that challenge.

GENERAL TIPS ON PUNCTUATION, GRAMMAR, AND USAGE

In this section, we've tried to identify and concentrate on the grammar problems that cause most of the errors that readers recognize. For example, if you split an infinitive or dangle a participle, you won't look nearly as bad as if your subject and verb don't agree or the reader can't tell where one sentence stops and the next one starts. If you want to delve into finer points of grammar and usage, many good books and style sheets are available.

Regardless of how you felt in elementary and high school English classes, the rules of grammar weren't designed to trip you up and make your life miserable. Actually, they are reasonable guidelines that serve as an orderly signal system to make sure that we are all making the same assumptions. Just as our understanding that a red light means "stop" avoids considerable chaos, so knowing some of the basic points of grammar enables us to communicate smoothly, efficiently, and effectively.

If you don't think correctness really matters in written communication, think again. A sloppily prepared document, no matter how compelling the argument, will give the audience an extra reason to disagree or simply disregard it. Being able to handle the language identifies you as an educated person. It's an indicator of your professionalism.

In most cases, rules of punctuation, usage, and mechanics are based on common sense. They help readers sort out information and break ideas up into logical units. In fact, if you avoid sentences longer than 17 to 20 words and write in the active voice, you won't have to be a grammarian to avoid most problems.

One word of caution: If you aren't sure of the difference between a complete sentence (independent clause) and a related group of words (clause or phrase), none of the rules for punctuation will make much sense. Remember that to be a sentence, a group of words must contain at least one independent clause.

One independent clause

> **Actor   Action   Receiver**
> The manager attended the meeting.

Two or more independent clauses

> **Independent Clause   Independent Clause**
> The manager attended the meeting, but the salespeople were out in the field.

One or more dependent clauses and one or more independent clauses

> **Dependent Clause   Independent Clause**
> Although the salespeople were out in the field, the manager attended the meeting.

PUNCTUATION

The Comma

Use a comma

- Before *and, but, or, for, nor, so, yet* (coordinating conjunctions) linking two sentences/independent clauses.

  The first-quarter earnings were down, but the company's future looks bright.

- After an introductory clause, phrase, or word.

  Although the meeting ended before noon, John and his supervisor . . . .

- To separate items in a series (*, and* signals the last item in a series).

  Her acceptance speech was dynamic, informative, and entertaining.

The Semicolon

You can write almost anything without ever using a semicolon. If you have problems keeping the rules straight, don't use it. If you think you've got the hang of it, here are a few pointers.

Use the semicolon

- Between closely related, short sentences.

    The plan will work; they've laid a strong foundation.

- When transitional expressions such as *however, therefore, moreover,* etc. connect independent clauses.

    The board approved the proposal that morning; however, a number of members were still arguing at lunch.

- Between long items in a series that contain commas (too many commas confuse the reader).

    We will increase productivity through dedication, creativity, and hard work; improve morale through better communication; and develop a strategic plan for strong, vigorous growth.

The Colon

The lead-in statement should be a complete sentence. What follows a colon can be another sentence, a phrase, or a bulleted list.

Use a colon

- To introduce a list.

    The company must offer the following insurance packages: hospitalization, major medical, dental, disability, and rehabilitation therapy.

- To link one statement to another when the second statement explains, emphasizes, or clarifies the first statement.

    We have one goal this year: to increase productivity.

- Following the salutation in a business letter.

    Dear Ms. Martinez:

The Apostrophe

The apostrophe is one of the most commonly misused punctuation marks.

Use the apostrophe

- To show possession.

  She undermined *George's* position in the meeting.

- To form contractions (when one or more letters are intentionally omitted).

  We *can't* wait any longer for a decision.

Don't use the apostrophe

- To form the plural of nouns, including acronyms (*PCs, Pontiac 6000s, System 36s*).

- To form the possessive of personal pronouns (*his, hers, ours, yours, theirs, its*).

Pay particular attention to the difference between *it's* (contraction for it is) and *its* (possessive of personal pronoun). If you have trouble with this one, put the contraction back in its original form and see if it still makes sense.

> *Example*
>
> Clearly Incorrect: The company has lost *it is* competitive advantage.
>
> Correct: The company has lost *its* competitive advantage.

AGREEMENT

Subject-Verb

Make sure that subjects and verbs agree in number (singular or plural).

- Don't be misled by words that come between the subject and its verb.

The *price* of the computers *keeps* a small business from having access to that network.

- Use a plural verb for subjects connected by *and.*

  Bob and George *are* both going to be out of town on Friday.

- If the subjects are joined by *or, nor,* or *not only . . . but also,* the verb must agree with the subject closest to it.

  Neither the president nor the sales managers *know* why she quit so suddenly.

  Neither the sales managers nor the president *knows* why she quit so suddenly.

- Use singular verbs for most indefinite pronouns such as *anybody, everybody, everyone, everything, somebody, each, no one.*

  No one here *knows* who the new president will be.

  Everyone *is* excited about the announcement.

- In inverted word order, the verb still must agree with the subject.

  What *are* the responsibilities of this position?

Pronoun-Antecedent

The *antecedent* is the noun, noun phrase, or other pronoun to which a pronoun refers. Pronouns must correspond to their antecedents in number (singular or plural.)

- Use a plural pronoun when antecedents are joined by *and.*

  The U.S. *and* Japan need to settle *their* differences and enter into mutually beneficial trade agreements.

- Use a singular pronoun when the antecedent is an indefinite pronoun.

  Everyone should turn *his* or *her* application in by Monday.

  Not:

  Everyone should turn their application in by Monday.

Generally speaking, we find devices such as "he or she" or "he/she" as a means to avoid gender bias awkward and irritating. In most cases, you can get less gender bias and more readability by recasting the sentence. One way to do this: Substitute a plural subject for the singular antecedent.

Example

All prospective employees should submit *their* applications by Monday.

Or better still:

If you want to apply for a job, be sure to submit *your* application by Monday.

Also look for ways to avoid singular antecedents like *either* or *neither* by emphasizing the common elements in the action the sentence describes. See the sentence under the next rule for an example.

- When antecedents are joined by *or* or *nor*, the pronoun must agree with the antecedent closest to it, if one is singular and the other is plural.

  Neither the CEO nor the vice presidents will put their careers on the line by making the tough decisions.

  Neither the vice presidents nor the CEO will tell you how he stands on the issue.

  Or in a gender-neutral form:

  The CEO and the vice presidents have tried to keep their jobs by avoiding tough decisions.

MECHANICS

Numbers

- Spell out numbers from one to nine and use figures for numbers 10 and above.
- Don't start a sentence with a number. If the sentence starts with a number, spell it out. Better yet, rearrange the sentence so that it starts with a word.
- If you have a number below 10 and one above 10 in the same sentence, use numbers for both.

- Always express the following in numbers:

  - Dates
  - Addresses
  - Page numbers
  - Percentages
  - Times with a.m. or p.m. after them
  - Temperatures
  - Money
  - Telephone numbers
  - Measurements
  - Scores
  - Decimals
  - Fractions

Capitalization

Use a capital letter for

- The first word of a sentence.
- The first word of a complete sentence that follows a colon.
- The first word of a displayed list, if what follows is a complete sentence. (If the items are not sentences, you may capitalize the first word or not. But be consistent).
- All important words in a title (everything except articles such as *a* and *the* unless they are the first word of the title, and short prepositions such as *in, of,* and *to*).
- Specific places such as political or geographical divisions.
- All personal names.
- Days of the week, months of the year.
- Personal titles, such as Ms., Dr., Senator.
- Abbreviations, if the words they stand for would be capitalized.
- The first letter of a quotation, unless you make it a part of your own sentence.
- Acronyms.
- Languages, nationalities.

USAGE

Words Commonly Confused

affect, effect

- Poor economic conditions *affect* sales dramatically. (Produce a change)
- The *effect* on the employees was devastating. (Something brought about by cause or agent)

capital, capitol

- We can't raise enough *capital* to retool the factory. (Money)
- What's going on in the *capitol* will affect all of us. (Government building)

cite, site, sight

- The government can *cite* the company with at least three violations. (Summon or quote)
- Is this the *site* of the new plant? (Location)
- He lost his *sight* as the result of an accident on the job. (Vision)

complement, compliment

- Their management styles *complement* each other. (Complete)
- The manager *complimented* her on her good work. (Praised)

conscience, conscious

- She operates the business as though she has no *conscience.* (Inner sense of right and wrong)
- The crew member was barely *conscious* when they pulled him from the wreckage. (Knowing, aware)

council, counsel

- The company CEO is a member of the city *council.* (A group)
- The legal *counsel* that we hired really dropped the ball on that one. (Advice, advisor)

human, humane

- The *human* resources director didn't attend the staff meeting. (People)
- Firing him just before the holidays wasn't a *humane* approach to the problem. (Having the best qualities of human beings)

incidence, incidents

- The *incidence* of white collar crime is rising steadily. (Degree of occurrence)
- The *incidents* I am going to tell you about will shock you. (Events)

lose, loose

- We can't *lose* that account. (Cut off, separate, mislay)
- He's like a *loose* cannon when he gets into a conflict. (Free, unrestrained)

moral, morale

- He has some real concerns about the *moral* implications of the new directive. (Generally accepted principle of right and wrong)
- Employee *morale* has never been higher. (Mental and emotional condition)

passed, past

- We have no record of his *past* employment. (In an earlier time)
- The company just *passed* last year's sales volume. (Went by)

personal, personnel

- She believes that she was fired for *personal* reasons. (Of a particular individual)
- The organization just doesn't have the *personnel* to do the job. (Persons employed)

perspective, prospective

- They need to look at the product from the customer's *perspective*. (Point of view)
- We have a *prospective* client visiting the office today. (Likely)

principle, principal

- It's the *principle* of the thing, rather than the money. (Rule or method)
- The *principal* reason for the improvement is the new reporting system. (First in rank)

rational, rationale

- That decision just wasn't *rational*. (In possession of one's reason)
- She never explained the *rationale* behind the logo. (Explanation of reasons)

respectively, respectfully

- First and second prizes went to Mary and Doug, *respectively*. (In order named)
- She *respectfully* submitted her resignation. (With due regard)

stationery, stationary

- Someone forgot to order new *stationery*. (Remember, paper ends in -er.)
- The engineers spent two hours deciding whether to use *stationary* or mobile cranes. (Stable)

too, to, two

- She has taken on *too* many assignments, *too*. (Excess and also)
- He has *to* go to L.A. this afternoon.
- They have *two* primary reasons for wanting to buy the company. (Number)

your, you're

- *You're* too emotional to deal with the issue. (Contraction for *you are*)
- You left *your* passport at the office. (Possessive pronoun)

Index

Communication strategy, development of, 3-16
Communication technology, developments in, 113-114
Completeness, of written document, checking for, 26-27
Conflicts, group, management of, 102-103
Credibility, 7
    in spoken communication, 60
Cross-hatching, avoidance of, 57

D

Data, processing of, for reader, 57
Decision maker, issues of concern to, and presentation planning, 68-69
Delays, telephone, minimizing, 90-91
Design
    appropriate, choice of, 39
    of document, 37-47
    of page, 42-44
    of presentations, 65-76
    of visuals, 49-58
Diagrams, 56
Discussion, during meeting, control of, 101-102
Distractions, during presentations, 76
Document, *see* Written document
Draft
    of group writing project, 105-107
    of written document, 25-26
Drawings, 55

E

Editing
    of group writing project, 105-107
    of written document, 35-36
E-mail, communication by, 113-114
Emergency equipment, for presentations, 76
Ending, of telephone communication, 90

Enthusiasm, in spoken communication, 61
Environment
    low-risk, for audience, creation of, 84
    presentation, control of, 74
Evidence, selection of, 10-11
Eye contact, with audience, 73-74

F

Fax, communication by, 113-114
Flow charts, 56
Font, selection of, 42-44
Format
    consistency in, checking for, 35
    of tables, 50-51
Furniture arrangement, for presentation, 75

G

Grammar, 36
    general tips on, 115-125
Graphic devices, 46-47. *See also* Visuals
Graphs
    bar, 51-52
    column, 51-52
    line, 53
Greeting, during telephone communication, 89-90
Group
    integrity of, support for, 102-103
    management of, during meeting, 101-102
Group communication, 97-104
Group presentations, 109-112
    difficulties of, 109-110
Group writing projects, management of, 105-107

H

Headings, creation of, 38-39
Highlighting techniques, 44-46
Hyphens, 44